"For over twenty years, I have been trying to attract the perfect friends and clients and I thought I was doing a pretty fair job until I read this book. I thought that I had to work my fingers to the bone to get enough contacts to weed through to find perfection. This book focuses the perspective for you and makes it seem effortless!"

—MAUREEN SANDERS
Vice President and Office Manager
Sterling Bank—Upper Kirby

"Finally the truth about how to attract the best customers (and keep them). *Attracting Perfect Customers* is a must-read for anyone exhausted or frustrated by the competitive, war-like race for customers and business success. You can relax a bit, breathe a sigh of relief, and exceed your goals with advice like this!"

—SHARON JORDAN-EVANS
coauthor of *Love 'Em or Lose 'Em:
Getting Good People to Stay* and
President, The Jordan Evans Group

"After being introduced to the Strategic Synchronicity process I have a clearer vision of the contribution I am to make in creating value for the customers, employees, and other stakeholders of Shell Services International. My Strategic Attraction Plans truly guide the most perfect people and events to me easily and effortlessly."

—PATTY WALTERS
Senior Consultant, Management Consulting,
Shell Services International, a part of the
Royal Dutch/Shell Group of companies

"A must-read if you've ever dreamed of having a 'perfect' client walk through the door! With clarity and precision, Hall and Brogniez teach us how to magnetize 'perfect' customers and rediscover a passion for our work."

—KATE LUDEMAN, PH.D.
President, Worth Ethic Corporation, and
coauthor of *The Corporate Mystic*

"A soulful approach to marketing yourself, your company, and what you love to do best. Essential reading for those who want to bring their spirituality to work."

—RICHARD BARRETT
business consultant and author of
Liberating the Corporate Soul:
Building a Visionary Organization

"Hall and Brogniez blend market analysis, intuition, visioning, planning, and plain old-fashioned persistence to create a practical, workable business strategy. Give their method a try and before you know it, you'll find yourself and your business transforming beyond belief!"

—C. LESLIE CHARLES
professional speaker and author of
Why Is Everyone So Cranky? and
The Customer Service Companion

"Wonderful book. Well thought through. Read it!"

—MICHAEL GERBER
author of the world-renowned E-Myth books
and Chairman and CEO,
E-Myth Worldwide

"I like the simplicity of the strategic model in *Attracting Perfect Customers*. The exercises brought forth insights and connections that helped me as I made changes in the work I do. I recommend this book."

—TOM HEUERMAN, PH.D.
writer/consultant

"This is an extremely significant book. It has altered my life. Imagine working only with clients you like and who like you. You can. How? Simple. Read this book and do what it says."

—MARTIN RUTTE
President, Livelihood, and coauthor of
Chicken Soup for the Soul at Work

"After ten years as a sales trainer, I couldn't agree more with the authors' guidelines on Strategic Synchronicity. They actually show us how to refocus our train of thought from 'how to find more customers' to 'attracting the perfect customer to us.' Their techniques prove that not only will we increase sales, but we will be able to service, retain, and provide an enjoyable sales environment for everyone."

—JERRY HOCUTT
President and Speaker for Hocutt & Associates, Inc.,
Home of the "Cold Calling For Cowards" Seminars
and FootInTheDoor.Com

"The authors state that 'it is possible to attract only customers who value your service, pay you what you are worth, and send referrals to your business or Web site on a regular basis.' If you would like this for your business, this book is for you."

—JUSTINE WILLIS TOMS
cofounder of New Dimensions Radio and
coauthor of *True Work: Doing What You Love
and Loving What You Do*

"Having been in business for over thirty years, I was surprised to learn of an approach to better marketing that I'd not heard before. I am clearly convinced that, by adopting the Strategic Synchronicity philosophy, all companies can improve their effectiveness and, more importantly, the bottom line. I am still amazed at the pure simplicity of the approach; but then aren't the best ideas always the simplest?"

—ROBERT W. FENN, PH.D.
Regional Director, Northeast Ohio Procurement
Technical Assistance Center,
Lake County Economic Development Center,
Lake Erie College

Attracting Perfect Customers

Attracting Perfect Customers

The Power of Strategic Synchronicity

Stacey Hall and Jan Brogniez

BERRETT-KOEHLER PUBLISHERS, INC.
San Francisco

Berrett-Koehler Publishers, Inc.
235 Montgomery Street, Suite 650
San Francisco, CA 94104-2916
Tel: (415) 288-0260   Fax: (415) 362-2512   www.bkconnection.com

ORDERING INFORMATION

Quantity sales. Special discounts are available on quantity purchases by corporations, associations, and others. For details, contact the "Special Sales Department" at the Berrett-Koehler address above.

Individual sales. Berrett-Koehler publications are available through most bookstores. They can also be ordered direct from Berrett-Koehler: Tel: (800) 929-2929; Fax: (802) 864-7626; www.bkconnection.com

Orders for college textbook/course adoption use. Please contact Berrett-Koehler:
Tel: (800) 929-2929; Fax: (802) 864-7626.

Orders by U.S. trade bookstores and wholesalers. Please contact Publishers Group West, 1700 Fourth Street, Berkeley, CA 94710. Tel: (510) 528-1444; Fax (510) 528-3444.

Printed in the United States of America

Printed on acid-free and recycled paper that is composed of 50% recovered fiber, including 10% postconsumer waste.

Library of Congress Cataloging-in-Publication Data
Hall, Stacey, 1965–
   Attracting perfect customers : the power of strategic synchronicity / by Stacey Hall and Jan Brogniez.
      p. cm.
   ISBN 1-57675-124-4
   1. Customer relations. I. Brogniez, Jan, 1965– II. Title.
HF5415.5.H26 2001
659.2—dc21   2001043561

Copyediting by PeopleSpeak.
Book design and composition by Beverly Butterfield, Girl of the West Productions.

FIRST EDITION
06 05 04 03   10 9 8 7 6 5 4

We dedicate this book to our
husbands and partners in life,
Bill Hall and Peter Brogniez,
our lighthouse keepers.

Contents

Foreword

Surely we've all had coincidences in our lives. We've been blessed with beat-the-odds, fortunate circumstances, and all we can do is shake our heads in wonder and be grateful that luck, serendipity, kismet—whatever we want to call it—came our way.

Stacey Hall and Jan Brogniez don't leave it at that. They think we can create our own luck. They believe we can increase the likelihood that synchronistic events will occur. They prove that clarity and commitment to values create a magnet that draws serendipity to us.

They don't just think, believe, and feel this. They've developed a system that shows us exactly how to do it, and they outline their ideas in an easy-to-understand, step-by-step way so we can implement them in our own lives.

Ready for some more good news? This book explains that marketing our self, our services, our products, or our organization does not have to be a hard sell. It does not have to be manipulative, pushy, or offensive—just the opposite.

Strategic Synchronicity is the perfect blend of yin and yang, head and heart, logic and intuition, initiative and patience. It's a system that appeals to left-brained individuals, who appreciate specific examples, and right-brained readers, who appreciate emotional and spiritual congruence.

I know these principles work because I've applied them in my own business for the past twenty years. Time and again I've picked up the phone (these days, logged on to e-mail), and the person on the other end has offered me something I've been wishing for: an opportunity to speak on a cruise, a consulting contract in a "slow" month, an endorsement from a best-selling author. These pleasant surprises weren't things I actively sought; they were by-products of a series of behind-the-scenes recommendations from people who have worked with me over the years and have become my "silent salespeople."

People who attend my workshops often tell me they wish they could have their own business, but they're not comfortable selling themselves. I reassure them that they won't have to if they do their job right. If they get really good at providing something people need, if they take responsibility for maintaining positive visibility, and if they do their best for every client every time, satisfied customers will become their best advertising.

If you apply the ideas in this book, you will receive benefits beyond your dreams. Opportunities will "fall into your lap" that defy the odds. People will come into your life offering exactly what you need or want at that time. And that's when you fulfill your end of the bargain by feeling grateful. As the authors point out, appreciating and acting on what comes our way is an integral part of this process. By behaving honorably, giving quality service, trusting this "invisible" process, and being thankful, you will be rewarded.

Attracting Perfect Customers: The Power of Strategic Synchronicity is a beneficial manual for anyone who wants to succeed in business—without ever lying. Read it and reap.

SAM HORN
President of Action Seminars
Author, *Tongue Fu!, ConZentrate,*
and *What's Holding You Back?*

Acknowledgments

Through the years, we have attracted an abundance of people who perfectly lit our way along the path toward creation of a new sales and marketing reality. It is with joy that we say thank you to each of them. Together, we acknowledge these extraordinary contributors to PerfectCustomers Unlimited and this book:

Zoe Jarboe—for preparing us to give birth to this book.

Sam Horn—for being the "midwife" for the message of Strategic Synchronicity.

Carolyn Fine—for holding our vision and keeping our profitability train on its track.

Sheryl Fullerton—whose enthusiasm and unerring instincts make her the most "perfect" literary agent, editorial consultant, and cheerleader.

Beverly Butterfield, Kathleen Epperson, Sharon Goldinger, B.J. Hateley, Tom Heuerman, Eileen Hammer, Maryanne Koschier, Andrea Markowitz, Karen Marquardt, and Paul Wright—whose editorial expertise and dynamic designs polished the book to its becoming a brilliant and valuable gem.

Maui Writers Conference staff—for making it possible for first-time authors to realize their dreams.

Steve Piersanti and the staff of Berrett-Koehler Publishers—for their mission of shifting business paradigms, transforming the publishing industry, and honoring each of its authors with their practices and collaborative spirits. With a special thank you to Richard Wilson for attracting the "perfect peacock" to our cover.

The following extraordinary women: Judy Adler and Linda Starr—for being our Muses and greatest teachers; Pamela Grant—for being committed to our greatest success; Ann Schroeder—for her appreciation of the magnitude of this message; Heather Smith—for her powerful stand for bringing our gifts to the world; Diana Petrocelli—for propelling us forward with her passion; and Patti Loegering Wendt—for her powerful stand for women being successful in business.

The following magnificent men: James Doyle—for his unwavering commitment to our success; Steve Gartrell—for creating the means for us to share effectively our message through the Internet; Monte Pendleton—who was the first to shine a light on our path; John Stringer—whose intrigue and interest expanded our capacity to create our methods as viable for global corporations; and Paul Turro—who stood for us having and living our dreams no matter what!

Our Landmark "community"—for supporting us in being all that we can be in the world.

And, to Lucki and Freddi (the cats)—our "purrfect" partners and whose playful spirits remind us to take time out for fun and nurturing ourselves.

On a personal note, Jan gives special thanks to her family for the joy they instill and particularly to her parents, Hazel and Al Stringer, and her daughter Jana, son-in-law Chad, and grandson Slade Knowlton. She also honors all the members of her family who "gave me an outstanding foundation upon which to live an extraordinary life." Stacey thanks and honors her parents, Janet and Elliot Rubenstein, and other members of her and Bill's family for "the wholeness and happiness they bring to my life and for their inspiring love and steadfast spiritual faith."

In addition, her gratitude is expressed to the members of the Universal House of Justice and the members of the Bahai International Community for the support, guidance, encouragement, and opportunities that each has provided on her developmental path and the several individuals she met who inspired her in those travels: James Bartee, Sabine Bredemeyer, Susan Clark, Danny Collins, Greg Cummins, Lea-Ann Gee, Chelly Goldberg, Margaret Griffith, Kirk Hokanson, the Jensen family, Beth Johnston, Nurith Kahane, Mary Kane, Linda and Peter Krivkovich, Susan Landwer, Lina Lou, Jeff and Pam Mondschein, Eileen and Milton Norman, Rolf Normann, Sylvia Padelford, Brenda Rarey, Tina and Phil Rose, Amelia Pawlak, Bob and Susan Rude, Sandi Salvo, Rita Schaaf, Smadar Svorai, Florence Towers, Marie Watts, Scott Weeden, the staff of The Message Company, the members of the National Speakers Association, the members of SpiritSystems, the staff of the University of Houston Small Business Development Center, and the members of the Houston Alumni Organization.

To our current and future "perfect" customers, we say thank you for transforming the world of business by first transforming your own companies into powerful magnets for attracting all the customers that you are meant to serve.

To each of our Synchronicity Leaders, we express our gratitude for connecting with this message and committing yourselves to share it with your own most perfect clients and customers.

In addition, we acknowledge and appreciate each of the people who have provided endorsements of our book. Thank you for providing us with your time, energy, and acknowledgments.

Introduction

Creating Synchronicity with Perfect Customers and Clients

HOW MANY times have you thought, "We need more customers"?

> If we don't change the direction we're going, we're likely to end up where we're headed.
>
> *Ancient Chinese proverb*

The vast majority of business owners and corporate executives believe that all of the problems in their businesses would be solved if they could just figure out the secret to finding more customers.

With this book, we are inviting you to partake of what owners, directors, and employees of successful businesses know: that it is essential to replace the thought "We need more customers" with the conviction "Our business now *attracts perfect customers only.*"

What Is a "Perfect" Customer?

Of course, we all know that there is no such thing as a perfect person. So how could there possibly be a perfect customer?

As we will explore further throughout this book, by our definition, a perfect customer is one whose needs are a perfect fit for a company's mission. When the relationship between need and service are perfectly aligned, positive results occur with amazing velocity and synergy—almost without effort.

A Perfect Customer Has the "Spark of Strategic Synchronicity"

Take a moment to picture one of your most "perfect" customers or clients—the one person with whom you enjoy or have enjoyed working. Is this person the perfect customer because he or she shows you respect and values your time? Does he or she trust that you have his or her best interests at heart? Does this perfect customer come to you with realistic expectations? Does he or she appreciate your efforts— happily paying what your product or service is worth and referring others to your company? Does working with this customer make you feel needed, appreciated, respected, and understood? Does he or she reconnect you with the passion and purpose that puts joy in your work—the very reason you began working in this company in the first place? Did this perfect customer come to you easily: did you feel an immediate sense of attraction and connection with this customer, as if fate brought you together at the perfect time and place? Did you feel as if you were the answer to this customer's prayers—the one for whom he or she had been searching—the perfect fit of need and solution?

How many of your customers are currently a perfect fit for your company? If the number is less than you wish, are you willing to believe that it is possible to create a profitable business that consists completely of customers who are attracted to doing business with you? Can you believe that it is possible to experience a "spark of Strategic Synchronicity" every time you begin a relationship with a new customer? Can you imagine it is possible to stand still and attract more than enough customers who value your service, pay you what you are worth, and send referrals to your business or Web site on a regular basis?

Not only is this possible, but it is as true for sole proprietorships as it is for Fortune 500 companies and for every size and type of business in between.

A Unique Marketing Model

We will introduce you to our Strategic Attraction Planning Process—a logical, practical, and unique model that is the catalyst for a new sales and marketing reality. It's a fundamental way of thinking that shifts how organizations are operated.

The Strategic Attraction Planning Process is designed to be used by business owners, corporate executives, and sales and marketing representatives. It is also meant to be used by receptionists, warehouse workers, engineers, technicians, lawyers, accountants—anyone at any level in an organization—because each has the power to attract or deflect "perfect" customers for the organization.

How Is the Strategic Attraction Planning Process Different from Other Marketing Models?

Traditional marketing models, which put emphasis on capturing market share and stealing customers away from competitors, require a business to adopt a mind-set of acquiring ever-larger numbers of customers. This never-ending search for more customers requires an abundance of people, time, and money, resources that are usually in short supply, even in the largest companies. For example, many dot-com organizations, with millions of dollars invested to assure their success, failed because their deep financial wells ran dry before the companies found enough actual customers to meet unrealistic sales projections.

Over the last ten years, numerous articles in magazines such as *Inc., Fast Company,* and *Sales and Marketing Management,* as well as a plethora of "relationship marketing" books, have been written to address the demise of so many companies as a result of this very dilemma. All of the research that has been compiled in these articles and books points to the fact that companies must spend less time on finding new customers and more time on defining their missions and values. Once the missions and values are identified, organizational structures and practices can be put in place to support the building of stronger relationships with the customers they are already serving. The equation: more clarity + more bonding = greater loyalty.

A long-held adage says that 20 percent of a business's customers account for 50 to 80 percent of the profits. With an increase of just 5 percent in the customer maintenance rate, according to a study conducted by Bain & Company, a Boston-based consultancy, a company can boost its profits by 25 to 95 percent.[1]

However, we ask the question, Why are only 20 percent of a company's customers considered to be "the best"? If these 20 percent account for the vast majority of profits, why does the company need the other 80 percent?

Rahul Jacob, in his *Fortune* magazine article "Why Some Customers Are More Equal Than Others," states that it has "always made *intuitive sense* to focus a company's resources on the best customers rather than on the flighty, fair-weather types."[2] We agree.

The next question is, Is it possible to build a business where every customer is "the best" or, as we would say, the "most perfect"? We say it is possible, and so do the hundreds of companies that have experienced the freedom of serving only perfect customers. It is also true that *everyone* working within an organization *already has the power* to attract these perfect customers, as well as to attract perfect employees, coworkers, vendors, and other stakeholders.

The Law of Attraction

The ability of each person to achieve strength and success with the Strategic Attraction Planning Process is drawn from a phenomenon of nature—the law of attraction. This phenomenon has been beautifully explained by noted consultants and educators Margaret J. Wheatley and Myron Kellner-Rogers in *A Simpler Way*. Their landmark book is an exploration into the question, How could we organize human endeavor if we developed different understandings of how life organizes itself? Wheatley and Kellner-Rogers find:

> There is an innate striving in all forms of matter to organize into relationships. There is a great seeking for connections, a desire to organize into more complex systems that include more relationships, more variety. This desire is evident everywhere in the cosmos, at all levels of scale.
>
> Particles are attracted to other particles and so create atoms. Microbes combine with other microbes to create capacities for larger organisms. Stars, galaxies, and solar systems emerge from gaseous clouds that swirl into coherence, creating new forms of energy and matter. Humans reach out to one another and create families, tribes, and work organizations.
>
> Attraction is the organizing force of the universe. Everywhere, discrete elements come together, cohere, and create new forms. We know one form of this attraction is gravity. No one knows what gravity is, but it is a behavior that permeates the universe. This behavior is ubiquitous attraction.
>
> Attraction has created the universe we know.[3]

Attraction can also be the fundamental building block for creating successful, fulfilling, and harmonious businesses. The power of attraction increases as we become clear about who we are and what we want. This clarity transforms us into powerful magnets, each automatically attracting others who have the same intention.

Quantum physicists, human behavior experts, and even health practitioners have proven that the universal law of attraction is sound. We, and hundreds of businesses, have proven for ourselves that applying this law of attraction to our sales and marketing practices easily brings to us compatible customers who fully appreciate the value of our products and services.

Now it's your turn to experience the *powerful spark of Strategic Synchronicity*. We invite you to research and explore these principles for yourself. We invite you to play with the Strategic Attraction Planning Process. We invite you to create your own Strategic Attraction Plan for serving more of your most perfect customers.

If you accept our invitation, then let's proceed.

Experiencing the Process

This is a how-to handbook for strategically applying the natural and universal law of attraction to the sales and marketing of your business as quickly as possible. We ask you to immerse yourself in the Strategic Attraction Planning Process by using the examples and exercises available to you in every chapter of this book. If you want to explore these concepts at an even deeper level, we have included a bibliography and a list of the resources that have supported us in our exploration.

The first step toward consciously engaging in this process of forming a greater degree of relatedness with your customers, employees, coworkers, and other stakeholders is to give up whatever attachment you may have to the commonly used and accepted marketing techniques that involve targeting customers. The second step is to prepare to refocus your efforts on your business mission, the true source of your powers of attraction. Each business mission is as unique and distinct as the people who create it, and the clearer you become about your business mission, the more effectively you and your company can attract your most perfect customers to your real or virtual doorstep.

In our experience, it is no longer necessary, logical, or productive to work eighty-hour weeks, struggling to stay ahead of the competition, because there is no race—not even in the fast-paced world of dot-coms. It is also no longer necessary to get to the marketplace first. Your most perfect customers are patiently waiting for you. In fact, *they are looking for you* and are counting on you to stand still so that they can find you at the most perfect time and place.

So your first exercise is to slow down. Take the time to both read and do the exercises in this book. You could read this book in a day. Yet our intention is that you will continue to experience the exercises, and the insights that they reveal, for years to come.

How to Use This Book

We can't stress this enough: The transformative power of this book lies in doing the exercises. Try each exercise on as if you were putting on a shirt for the first time. You won't know if it fits unless you are inside it. If it's too tight or uncomfortable, take it off—then try on another one until you discover those exercises that are a "perfect fit" for you.

To assist you on your journey of exploration, we've organized our book into three sections:

- Part I—The Six Standards of Strategic Synchronicity
- Part II—The Strategic Attraction Planning Process

- Part III—Strategic Attraction in Action: Twenty-One
  Daily Tips

In part I, you will begin to play with the six building blocks that cause the Strategic Attraction Planning Process to produce *Strategic Synchronicities*. In part II, you will be guided through the creation of your first Strategic Attraction Plan, the plan that re-creates your organization into a powerful and unwavering lighthouse, attracting perfect customers to its shore. Through the tips and exercises in part III, the intensity and breadth of your illumination will be greatly increased, and with that increase will come a corresponding increase in your organization's powers of attraction.

According to Dr. Robert Fenn, regional director of the Northeast Ohio Procurement Technical Assistance Center, an economic development center: "Having been in business for over thirty years, I was surprised to learn of an approach to better marketing that I'd not heard before. I'm surprised because it seems so obvious. But, as we all know, the devil is in the details. I am clearly convinced that by adopting the Strategic Synchronicity philosophy, all companies can improve their effectiveness and, more importantly, the bottom line. I am still amazed at the pure simplicity of the approach; but then aren't the best ideas always the simplest!"[4]

Throughout this book, you will be introduced to many Synchronistic Perspectives provided by thought leaders—corporate executives, staff members of organizations, and entrepreneurs—all of whom have been experimenting with this process and who have voiced their own experiences with these same exercises. If you find that a spark of Strategic Synchronicity occurs with any or all of them, you are encouraged to contact them directly. Each one has volunteered to be a resource of advice and encouragement for those of you just beginning your exploration. You will find contact information in the Resources section at the end of this book.

One last note about how to use this book. You will notice the use of the word "perfect" over and over again. This is done intentionally. Behavior therapists have proven that a new behavior more quickly becomes a habit when the behavior is repeated frequently. So we give you many opportunities to play and practice with the term "perfect."

In the process of adjusting to the term, our clients have often asked if "perfect" can be replaced with some other word, such as "ideal" or "desired." We understand that the concept of perfection makes some people uncomfortable because many of us have been taught that no one is perfect. We ask you to resist the temptation to exchange the word for another, more comfortable yet less specific, word.

Let's begin the practice of attracting perfect customers now.

PART I

The Six Standards of Strategic Synchronicity

> Lighthouses speak to vigilance. They speak to caring. They speak to being there. They speak to helping other human beings.
>
> *Peter Ralston*

HOW TO create a "perfect connection" with more customers, and recognize it at the moment it is occurring, is the ultimate goal of the journey on which you are about to embark.

Your first stop on this journey is to acquaint yourself with the six affirming standards for conducting business in the new millennium. Daily practice of these Strategic Synchronicity Standards will lay the foundation for a more prosperous, profitable, productive, and perfect business environment.

It is on this foundation that you will create your own Strategic Attraction Plan, a strategic process that works so quickly—usually within two days—that the results appear almost like coincidental occurrences, or "synchronicities."

According to *Merriam-Webster's Collegiate Dictionary,* "synchronicity" is defined as "the coincidental occurrence of events and especially psychic events (as similar thoughts in widely separated persons or a mental image of an unexpected event before it happens) that seem related but are not explained by conventional mechanisms of causality."

Our definition of "Strategic Synchronicity" is different in that we believe it is possible to both design and identify the process that causes the resulting relationship. Through our years of training people at hundreds of entrepreneurial organizations and corporations, as well as nonprofit and governmental organizations, in the Strategic Attraction Planning Process, we have found that it is strategically possible to attract relationships that begin with a high level of connectedness—a *powerful* spark of Strategic Synchronicity—and that produce the most enriching, satisfying, and prosperous ongoing exchanges of information and energy.

The Lighthouse Test

How can you tell if you and your company are strategically ready to attract only the "most perfect" customers to serve? By using the simple Lighthouse Test.

Imagine a lighthouse standing strong and tall on the rocky shore of a beautiful harbor. The water is calm, the sky is blue, and many boats are out at sea. But off in the distance a storm cloud is forming. It approaches the shore very quickly. The sky is getting darker, the waves are getting rougher, and many of the boats are being tossed about on the water. As the rain and the wind pick up strength, the power of the beam of light emanating from the lighthouse increases. The darker the skies become, the brighter the light shines to provide safety and security in the midst of the storm.

Notice that not all of the boats need this beam of light to guide them to safety. Some have more confident captains and crews, and some are fully equipped to manage through storms safely and effectively. Now imagine that the lighthouse gets upset because some of the boats are choosing to follow their own path. The lighthouse feels that it is not successful if its light is not guiding all of the boats in the sea. It sprouts arms and legs and runs up and down the beach acting like a searchlight, doing its best to catch the attention of all the boat captains, attempting to encourage more of them to depend on its light.

What do you think would be the result?

Most likely, the boats whose captains were depending on a steady, constant stream of light to guide them safely around potential dangers would be damaged or destroyed in the chaos and confusion. Other boats might be steered dangerously close to shore so those on board could get a better look at the spectacle. Still others would be perfectly content to stay where they are—out at sea, relying on their own navigational equipment. The result: very few boats would be served well or at all by the lighthouse.

Here's the test.

How often are you, your employees, and your coworkers operating like lighthouses standing securely on the shore, attracting and safely guiding the boats (customers) that need your business with your light? How often do you run up and down the beach frantically looking for boats (customers) to serve?

Perfect Customers Are Most Likely to Find You When You Are Standing Still

It takes a lot of energy to look for people to serve. More than likely you have had the experience of trying to figure out how you could find the greatest number of customers. You spent much time and money experimenting, looking for the right way to catch their attention. Once you caught their attention, you had to convince them that you are the one who has what they want. By the time you actually found someone willing to try what you have to offer, you were exhausted!

So when a customer told you that he was not completely satisfied with your products, your policies, or your pricing, you were more than willing to make compromises to satisfy him. Truth be known, you were just too tired to put up a fight. Thinking that you won the war, you felt you could afford to let him win this smaller skirmish—especially in light of what it would cost you to go out and hunt down another customer to replace this one.

If you'd had greater confidence and financial resources, you might have been more willing to listen to your tiny inner voice, the one that speaks for your instincts, which said, "Be careful. This one could be more trouble than he's worth. This customer is not meant for you."

Instead, you convinced yourself that this customer must be meant for you because he responded to your advertising or clicked on your hyperlink. You were afraid that if you didn't serve him, the competition would. Of course, your inner voice was right. By the time you ended your tortured relationship with this customer, you knew that no amount of money in the world would be enough to compensate you for the exhausting cost of the experience.

This is the typical end result when you buy into the adversarial marketing school of thought that preaches a gospel of "targeting audiences," "stealing market share," and "eliminating the competition." These "stealth" strategies virtually guarantee that if you do win the battle, you will end up with customers who will be impossible to satisfy because they are not a perfect fit for your company. What you are "winning" with these strategies are another company's perfect customers.

While it is easy to blame the customer for the poor quality of the interaction, it is important to remember that you are solely responsible for choosing to serve a customer whose needs are not a perfect match for your company.

The lesson to be learned from this type of experience is to listen for and trust your inner voice when you encounter a less-than-perfect customer. It's warning you that your own distinctive light has gone out or that perhaps you forgot that lighthouses do not wade out into the water looking for boats to serve. Your responsibility is to stand still and keep shining your own distinctive light, to keep polishing the lens to ensure that your light has the power and brilliance to break through the darkness and attract the attention of only perfect customers.

The following six chapters introduce the six Strategic Synchronicity Standards. These standards provide essential training in how to stand still so that your most perfect customers can come straight to your shore, your door, or your Web site.

1

Be on Purpose with Your Mission

A FEW years ago, while working at a job that she did not
enjoy, Stacey came across the
following affirmation: "Do what
you love to do and the universe
rushes in to support you." She

> Work is evolving from
> supporting only our survival
> to nourishing and
> encouraging our livelihood.
>
> *Martin Rutte*

realized as she read the statement that she did not feel supported by
the universe in her job. Rather than being easily swept along to her
goals, she felt as if she were constantly walking into a windstorm.
Each day seemed harder than the day before. Although she originally
thought the company's mission and values were aligned with her own,
it became apparent that she had been fooling herself. In giving the
organization what it needed, she was increasingly surpressing her
own needs. Yet she was attached to the job because she wanted the
salary, prestige, and connections that came with it.

As a community service, she would periodically conduct free workshops to teach marketing and communications principles to business
owners. She truly loved facilitating the workshops, and the people who
attended let her know how much they enjoyed her teaching methods.

She felt completely alive when she was leading those workshops. Her personal mission—assisting organizations to operate in the best interests of the community—had found a voice. When she read that affirmation, the realization that these workshops were her business mission, her unique service to the world, hit her like a thunderbolt!

She had a choice: continue to fight against the wind until it finally blew her away, or allow herself to be carried along by the wave of certainty and joy that she had a responsibility to share her unique understanding of marketing with the world.

Just one problem stood in the way of making what was otherwise such a clear choice—money. She had to ask herself why she was making her workshops available for free. The answer was that she was not sure anyone would attend if she charged for them. She realized that she would be stuck in an unfulfilling job as long as she lacked trust that she could make money doing what she loved to do. With that realization, she knew that it was time to open her own consulting practice and be "on purpose" with her mission.

Richard Barrett, visionary, consultant, and best-selling author, recently spoke about his work supporting leaders in building values-driven organizations. At the end of the session, when one member of the audience thanked him for his insights, Richard responded, "I am grateful to be a channel for this information—and I thank God that this is the way I get to make my living." In that one sentence, Richard summed up what each of us who is truly living our passion gets to feel about our business.

It is our belief that most successful businesses began with someone's passionate mission: to share new information, produce a better product, provide a new understanding, contribute to the culture. A successful business remains successful because it stays true to its mission. How does a business stay true to its mission?

- By becoming clear about whom it is meant to serve
- By hiring only people who are truly aligned with the mission
- By ensuring its products, its management practices, and its organizational structures are all in alignment with the mission
- By measuring how well the organization has achieved its mission each and every day
- By trusting that money is a natural by-product of staying true to the mission

A business that stays true to its mission is an "attractive" business. An attractive business is one that is standing still and solid, emanating the light of its mission, so that its most perfect customers can easily find their way to the company.

Is the Customer Always Right?

Businesses with an overactive appetite for short-run results—created from a desire to grab the greatest number of customers in order to make the most money in the least amount of time—are much like the frantic lighthouse described above. Running up and down the beach, these businesses soon get winded and deplete their energy.

Their attractiveness quickly fades because this least-common-denominator approach lacks the depth of a more sophisticated *strategic* understanding of how to build longer and more satisfying relationships. A slower, surer reliance on the process of attraction allows a business to expand from its capacity to serve appropriate, appreciative customers who respond to the company's intent and mission without having to be "sold," "baited," or "snatched away" from the competition.

While nothing is inherently wrong with the old approach, it does require a business to expend a great deal of time, energy, and money on developing tools to predict every possible customer need and desire. It also has to prepare for "damage control," to handle the many complaints that come when its predictions are inaccurate.

Conversely, when the owner, managers, and employees design the business out of their mutual goals and shared values, they know exactly which types of customers the business is suited to serve. They know exactly which services and products they desire to provide to these customers. They know the business's hours of operation, they know the size of the staff, and they know what to charge for the products and services.

This information comes directly from asking themselves, "How would I want to be served by this business?" They trust that their mission is to serve others in just the way they would want to be treated. This means standing absolutely secure in the knowledge that many others need to receive their services or products. The energy that emanates from such confidence is like the light that shines from a lighthouse.

As the sky becomes dark, the light in the lighthouse automatically turns on. That is its mission. It does not wait for a boat to arrive before shining its light. It never waivers from its function of being a lighthouse, even if no boats are in the harbor on a particular night.

A perfect example of the concept of designing and maintaining a business committed to its mission is shown in *The Nordstrom Way: The Inside Story of America's #1 Customer Service Company*, written by Robert Spector and Patrick D. McCarthy. Nordstrom's mission— "Not service like it used to be, but service that never was. A place where service is an act of faith"—encourages entrepreneurial, motivated men and women to operate from their own personal missions in making an extra effort to provide customer service that is unequaled in American retailing. If revenue is an indicator of how true a company stays to its mission, then Nordstrom, with sales in excess of $4 billion, is solidly secure and a very "attractive" company.[5]

What Are You Bringing to the World?

The key to staying fully passionate about your business and fully empowered is to ensure that your personal mission and your business mission are completely aligned. Whether you own, manage, or work for your company, you as an individual have a personal mission. Are you clear about what it is? Do you know what you want to bring into the world each day?

We had the pleasure of working with Bambi McCullough, senior vice president of the Houston-based Sterling Bank, and her fellow executives in aligning their personal missions with the organization's business mission— "Exceptional People Providing Unexpected Personal Service." With the vision of becoming the number one bank in the country for owner-operated businesses, they are delivering on their mission through these six service standards, which define what customers can expect from each and every employee:

1. To make every day our grand opening.

2. To Listen, Listen, Listen.

3. To serve others the way we want to be served.

4. To fulfill the customers' needs and exceed their expectations.

5. To be appreciative and respectful.

6. To be confident, knowledgeable, and continue to learn.

Each time Ed Young, owner of Edwin G. Young II Insurance Agency, serves his most perfect customers, he has a clear sense of how closely his personal and business missions are aligned. He proudly displays his unique mission in his e-mail signature line "Your Friendly Farmers Agent and Reconstructionist: When tragedy strikes, we help you reconstruct your life with dignity."

To know if your business is aligned with your personal mission, you must first be aware of your personal mission. One way to construct a *personal* mission statement is to start by distinguishing the values that you hold closest to your heart. Your core values are those qualities and principles by which you measure your integrity. They give you a foundation to stand upon.

Rick Sidorowicz, editor of *The CEO Refresher*, referencing the work of James Collins and Jerry Porras in "Building Your Company's Vision," gives a concise and complete overview of the nature of these core values, whether they are held by a person or an organization:

> Core values are the organization's sense of character or integrity. Core values define what an organization stands for. Values are "core" if they are so fundamental and deeply held that they will change seldom, if ever. On the other hand it is more likely that the organization will change markets if necessary to remain true to its core values.
>
> Perhaps the key to "greatness" in the sense of viability, adaptability, longevity, and relevance for organizations is this sense of character, identity, unwavering purpose, integrity and the core values that you truly stand for. You discover core ideology by looking inside. It has to be authentic. You can't fake it. It's meaningful only to people inside your organization and it need not be exciting to others outside.
>
> How do you get people to share your core values? You don't. You can't. Just find people that are "predisposed" to share your values and purpose, attract and retain those people, and let those who don't share your values go elsewhere. [6]

Take a moment now to write down in the space below the values that are at your core. Feel free to create your list with a partner with whom you can bounce ideas back and forth.

To get you started, you might want to consider the following core values—integrity, joyfulness, confidence, dedication, a sense of humor, commitment, spirituality, honesty, service, leadership—and add some of them to your list. Next, consider what other values are important to you, and add them to the list below.

My Core Values

1.

2.

3.

4.

5.

6.

7.

8.

9.

From this list of core values, select the three or four that are the most important to you.

Next, arrange these values into a mission statement. For example, if you selected joyfulness, honesty, dedication, and service, your sentence might be "My personal mission is to ensure that I bring honesty, dedication, and service joyfully into everything I do for others."

You may feel that one value is more important to you than all the rest. For example, you may believe that the most important value is justice—that without justice, nothing else matters. If that is the case, then your mission statement might be "My personal mission is to ensure that everyone is treated with justice."

Now you have a basis from which to determine if your business is also operating from this mission. Are the core values of the business you own, you manage, or that employs you in alignment with your core values?

If your answer is yes, you have a solid foundation on which to create your Strategic Attraction Plan for more perfect customers.

If not, we encourage you to use the Strategic Attraction Planning *Process* provided in part II to attract a more perfect job for you, one that is aligned with your core values and your mission.

Vibrant Businesses Are More Attractive

Why is it so important for your personal and business missions to be fully aligned? With this alignment, you stand taller, your light shines farther, and you are more vibrant, more clearly visible, and much more attractive to the customers who are most perfect for you to serve. This is what it means to be on purpose with your mission. Now let's explore in detail whom and what you want to attract.

2

You Have the Power to Attract
Whatever You Desire

> Manifesting—the business of doing nothing more than bringing into form a new aspect of yourself.
>
> *Wayne W. Dyer*

IF YOU can envision it, you can manifest it. It's that simple.

Recent studies in the area of quantum physics have resulted in a growing understanding and acceptance of the concept of "mind over matter," that we can control the outcome of events by concentrating on changing our current thought patterns and envisioning the outcome that we prefer. Numerous consultants, behavior therapists, and authors have expounded on the practice and process of manifestation. Two such proponents are Wayne Dyer and Eileen Caddy.

In his book *Manifest Your Destiny,* Dyer shares his experience that "the process of creation begins first with a desire. Your desires, cultivated as seeds of potential on the path of spiritual awareness, can blossom in the form of freedom to have these desires in peace and harmony with your world. Giving yourself permission to explore this path is allowing yourself the freedom to use your mind to create the precise material world that matches your inner world."[7] Dyer is reminding us that what we sow with our thoughts, we reap in the physical world.

Eileen Caddy's Findhorn Community on the northernmost coast of Scotland is internationally known for growing an abundance of plants, vegetables, fruits, and herbs, *even in the worst possible conditions.* Caddy attributes her green thumb to her philosophy of expectations: "Expect your every need to be met, expect the answer to every problem, expect abundance on every level, expect to grow spiritually. You are not living by human laws. Expect miracles and see them take place. Hold ever before you the thought of prosperity and abundance, and know that your doing so sets in motion forces that will bring it into being."[8]

You have undoubtedly heard stories of people training their minds to overcome personal and physical obstacles, healing themselves of life-threatening illnesses, for example. These breakthroughs have opened the door for us to use this process in healing our businesses as well. First of all, it is time to recognize that marketing is, and was always intended to be, about envisioning and then attracting to us those customers who are perfect for our business to serve.

It's time to shift our thinking about our businesses from a "scarcity" model—where there are not enough customers to go around—to a model of abundance. We must turn our attention away from the schools of thought that have taught us that good customers are difficult to find, that we have to steal them from our competitors, and that we have to keep meeting our customers' ever-increasing and outrageous demands in order to keep them as our customers. As long as this is what we believe business to be, this is the kind of business we will create. In fact, this idea has become a self-fulfilling prophecy for most businesses.

"Synchronicity Strategists," practitioners of the Strategic Synchronicity marketing model, know that their business magnetism (and profit) grows when they simply focus their attention on envisioning perfect customers flocking to their doors on a regular basis.

"How could it possibly be that easy?" you may ask. Consider this: if a picture is worth a thousand words, then one's vision speaks volumes in attracting those qualities and attributes that one desires to have in a perfect customer, coworker, employee—even a spouse.

We All Have a Natural Ability to Attract

We all have the ability to think a thought and have it manifest itself quickly. Perhaps you have had an experience similar to the one that Jan had while attending an industry conference soon after accepting a position as vice president of sales for a telecommunications company. Jan was gripped by fear as she approached the hotel ballroom, which was already filled with more than 3,000 people, almost all of them complete strangers to her. Taking a few minutes to regain her composure, she thought about her goal of attracting new prospects for her company. She decided to turn the attraction process into a game. She stood in a uncrowded section of the room and began to visualize the type of people she wanted to attract—presidents and top executives of companies, decision makers, and others who had a wide circle of influence. Within five minutes of Jan's achieving this clarity of vision, a man approached her and introduced himself. He was the president of his company and very well connected in the industry. His company was also a very loyal client of Jan's company. Upon learning that Jan was new to the industry, he made it his responsibility throughout the evening to introduce her to the decision makers of many other companies, who soon became her clients—exactly as she had visualized!

The key to experiencing Strategic Synchronicity on a consistent basis is to prepare yourself to receive what you desire. One of the preparation steps is to envision what it would feel like and look like to receive what you desire. To learn how, practice this exercise.

Take a deep breath and then another one. During the next two minutes, imagine a steady stream of *perfect* customers coming to your door or calling you on the phone or visiting your Web site. Do not let yourself worry about how you are going to serve them all. Simply allow yourself to envision this abundance of customers. Imagine these customers requesting your services, handing you large amounts of money, smiling at you with pleasure at having found your company. Bask in the glory of this vision.

Are you able to envision perfect customers streaming through your doors? Or are you envisioning thousands of visitors logging on to your Web site? Or maybe you are envisioning all of your phone lines lit up with perfect customers, each calling to place an order.

At the end of these two minutes is your energy restored? Are you feeling like a dynamo? Can you sense the power of attraction?

Perhaps you are now a little further along your path to becoming a Synchronicity Strategist, as was Tom Heuermann, a consultant from Colorado, after he tried this exercise: "I actively did this—and the two minutes flew by. I ended up with a new vision for my Web site home page."[9]

If you are not feeling elated, then perhaps you let a few less-than-perfect customers sneak into your vision and spoil the picture. If that is the case, then you may want to repeat the exercise, being careful to envision only customers that are a perfect fit for your products and services so that you can serve an abundance of them easily and effortlessly.

Before proceeding to chapter 3, we encourage you to allow yourself to revel in this vision.

3

Like Attracts Like:
Whom Do You Like?

> Pay any price to stay
> in the presence of
> extraordinary people.
>
> *Mike Murdock*
> The Leadership Secrets
> of Jesus

VINCE LOMBARDI once said, "Confidence is contagious. So is lack of confidence." That is, like attracts like—confidence attracts confident customers. The power of attraction lies in this principle of reciprocity. When we value ourselves and our business, potential customers are also able to see the value.

For your business to be its most attractive to others, start believing in yourself. When you believe in yourself, you will attract more people who also believe in you. These are the ones who are happy with your hours of operation, who find that you charge a fair price in exchange for full value, who bring others to your Web site. In short, when you feel good about you, then you will attract customers who appreciate you. Imagine your business consisting of only these types of customers. Imagine how easy it would be to serve them, no matter how their numbers might multiply. They would all be happy with your hours, your prices, and your policies and procedures, and their suggestions for improvement would only make your job easier.

If this sounds like a pipe dream, then keep reading. Part II gives specific instruction on how to create a Strategic Attraction Plan that will bring in customers who are perfect for you. This also applies to attracting perfect employees and other perfect stakeholders.

Do You Like Your Business?

We learned firsthand the importance of fully valuing our business so that others can value it, too. We decided to provide a complimentary service to our clients by creating an on-line bulletin board where they could post announcements every week to promote their businesses around the world. The guidelines for posting were very simple: Write the announcement as you wish it to appear, use proper grammar, keep it to two paragraphs in length, and submit it by Wednesday for Friday posting. However, over the course of a few months we noticed that the guidelines were being disregarded. Announcements were arriving after the Wednesday deadline, and they were sent with typos and poor grammar. Lengthy announcements were sent as attachments with a request for us to edit them. Our enjoyment for providing this service was diminishing quickly. We were ready to stop providing it, yet we were getting great satisfaction from facilitating these global connections between Synchronicity Strategists.

It suddenly occurred to us that our frustration came from the impression that our subscribers, in their carelessness, were indicating a lack of appreciation for this service.

Since we believe that how each of us views others is simply a reflection of our own behavior, we realized that we were not fully valuing our own service. We had let it become a chore instead of a labor of love. We were not treating the bulletin board like a precious commodity. And when we started taking our efforts for granted, so did those we wanted to serve. The minute we began spending time and energy to upgrade the look and features of the bulletin board to make it visually more appealing, we began attracting an abundance of announcements. Once again, the announcements began arriving on time. They were well written. And the subscribers followed our editorial format, so despite the increase in volume, the bulletin board took *less* time to manage.

Consider where in your business you might be taking yourself, your products, or your services for granted. Where do you feel that others are not fully appreciative of what you have to offer?

What did you enjoy doing in the past that now feels like a chore? Why does it feel like that? When did it start to feel like a chore?

Once you have answered these questions, ask yourself how you could increase your appreciation of yourself and your business. What changes, upgrades, or revisions could you make that would improve this area and make it more attractive to you and to others? Perhaps a service should be discontinued. If you were to decide to discontinue this service, how would that make your business more attractive? Where would you prefer to put the extra time, energy, and resources?

By clearly recognizing the tangible value of your services and your company, you automatically increase your capacity to attract perfect customers, employees, investors, vendors, and other stakeholders.

Perfection Is in the Eye of the Beholder

> You are the same today that you are going to be
> five years from now except for two things: the people
> with whom you associate and the books you read.
>
> —*Charles Jones*

You always have a choice as to whom you bring into your life. You can always, at any time, define who is most fitting for you to have in your business, in your social settings, in your life.

The principle behind the concept of a perfect customer or perfect employee lies in asking, What is a *perfect match* for me? Said another way, Whom do I *deserve to have* in my life?

Each of us gets to say who or what is a perfect match for ourselves. What is perfect for one person is not necessarily perfect for another. You are the only one who knows what is perfect for you.

When our customers first hear us speak about this concept, they often say that they don't know what is perfect for them. Our answer is always the same: We all know what is *not* perfect for us. For example, it may not be perfect for you to have an employee who comes late to work every day. It may not be perfect for you to have a customer who does not pay in a timely manner for a product or service that you provide. Once you start considering what is *not* perfect, you will find that you can develop a long list of characteristics.

When you have recognized what is not perfect or is less than perfect, you can determine what is perfect for you by simply identifying the opposites of these characteristics. For example, it is not perfect for us to work with customers past 5:00 P.M. Monday through Thursday. We deserve to complete our work by 5:00 P.M. in order to have healthy, full, and balanced lives. So we declare that perfect clients support us in completing our work by 5:00 P.M. each workday.

Creating a Strategic Attraction Plan

When you make a list of items that you desire and deserve to have in your business and your life, you are starting to create a Strategic Attraction Plan. As we explored in chapter 1, this planning process begins with the alignment of your personal and business missions.

As you develop plans to improve and enhance the quality of each of the relationships in your life, you become more clear and aware of how you deserve to be treated in these relationships. More importantly, you also become more aware of how you want others to expect to be treated and served by you. As Gary Young, the president and CEO of Avela Corporation, writes, "I find it helpful to develop a mission-specific statement as it pertains to a few high-profile clients and let them know how I am developing the future as it pertains to them. My mission for my clients is to grow in ways that serve them and us. One of the first things I ask to know about a potential client is their mission statement to ensure that it is in alignment with mine."[10]

You, too, have a specific mission to offer a better, more efficient, or more cost-effective product or service to the community. Your business will falter and fail when you forget to stay focused on your particular mission. And you will lose your focus if you take the attitude that you will serve anybody and everybody. Your mission is to serve only those who want what you are best at providing. While good ideas can come from customer requests, the trick is to know if it's a good idea for *you*. When a customer asks you to lower your prices, to provide a service that you don't truly want to provide, or does not appreciate what you have to offer, remember, that is not your perfect customer!

What Do You Desire to Have in Your Business?

Play with the question of what you want in your business by embarking on a treasure hunt. Here are your instructions:

1. Acknowledge that each person you meet today has at least one perfect quality, a quality that you find attractive.

2. Your objective is to find that quality.

3. As soon as you identify the perfect quality, write it down.

At the end of the day, your list may look like this:

- Has a nice smile
- Gave me a compliment

- Provided me with a referral
- Has a very organized office
- Dresses fashionably
- Makes great cookies
- Said "thank you"

These qualities are your treasures and the beginning of your list of what you desire to have in your life and your business. These are your declarations of what is perfect for you to have and attract. You may wish to play the game again tomorrow. Feel free to play it every day. You are limited only by how much treasure you can stand to amass.

If you play the game more often, you will notice that perfect people will start popping up everywhere. You may find that you have an experience similar to Kit Lutz, an independent beauty consultant with Mary Kay Cosmetics. She reports, "Yesterday at a BNI (Business Network International) meeting, I was drawn to one of our guests. Of all things, she is a chiropractor; she gave me advice on my back, which has been causing me great pain. She told me that she had sold Mary Kay about five years ago, so I asked her to attend our next meeting. She is now a customer of mine and is just exactly the quality of person that I want all of my customers to be. At the meeting, she told my team leader that there was just something about me that drew her to me."[11]

J. Richard Stanley, president of My Printer, reports a similar experience: "One day after all of my staff had departed, a customer came in to pick up her order. We had not met before, so she did not know that I was the owner of My Printer. She shared how much she appreciated David (our graphic artist) putting forth more effort than what she expected and that the final result was everything she hoped for. I was a bit taken aback. It has been so rare that compliments like hers have been volunteered. The dialogue that followed was warm and unguarded. It was so uplifting! After three days, this heightened sense of enthusiasm is still with me." [12]

As you create and develop your own Strategic Attraction Plan, you will also experience the ease with which you attract perfect customers, employees, investors, and more. You can attract virtually any type of person that is perfect for you to have in your life and your business—if you are willing to do so and if you believe that you deserve to attract what you desire.

4

Choose Collaboration, Not Competition

> Great partnerships are characterized by generosity—an abundance mentality and a giving attitude that willingly, even eagerly, go beyond the basic requirements.
>
> *Chip R. Bell and Heather Shea*
> Dance Lessons

THE BASIC assumptions upon which traditional marketing approaches are built are ready for updating. For example, if we asked whether businesses actually have to compete for customers, the answer would certainly be "Of course, they do!" But there is an alternative perspective, an approach that can create a dramatic shift, not just in the way business is done but in how we treat our customers and each other.

This is the perspective of collaboration, which carries the implication that each of us is unique, that no two people are exactly alike. If no two people are exactly the same, then it stands to reason that no two businesses are exactly alike. It is simply not possible for two businesses to serve the same client's needs equally. One will be a better fit than another; the best fit produces a perfect client or customer working with the perfect provider.

The Idea of Perfect Fit

Each of us, and the businesses we've joined or created, exists for a specific purpose or mission. Our businesses have developed as a result of our own experiences and needs and are simply tools for fulfilling our missions. Each business has its own mission to serve a particular group of customers in a particular way. That is why businesses have no need to compete with each other in the way we've traditionally thought of competition. Instead, business owners and managers could collaborate in ways that truly serve their customers' and their own interests. If this sounds heretical, then it shows how deeply the concept of competition— "survival of the fittest"—colors our views of the way we do business.

Consider the memorable scene in the classic movie *Miracle on 34th Street* when Kris Kringle, as Santa Claus at Macy's, refers a customer to Gimbels, a rival department store, because he knows that the customer will find the exact item she is looking for there. Kringle recognizes that it is in Macy's best interests to serve the needs of the customer—even if it means losing a sale to another retailer. He knows that he is helping to build a reputation among customers that Macy's is the first place to shop for superior service.

Today, when consumers have an abundance of choices in products and distribution outlets, businesses can shine even brighter— and be of greatest service to themselves, their clients, and their communities—when they are knowledgeable about the products and services offered by other businesses in their own and related industries. Consumers value services that save them time, money, and headaches. By becoming this type of resource through collaborating with others in your industry, you increase the overall abundance of products and services and will ultimately bring the greatest success to everyone. When you put your focus on a broad-based vision, then the odds of success for your own business increase dramatically.

How do you know when a customer is a perfect fit for you and your business? You recognize a perfect customer the moment you meet one. An immediate spark of attraction and connection between this person and you quickly leads to mutual admiration. Almost instantly, you find yourself freely sharing information with this customer because you feel needed, appreciated, respected, and understood. You find that your opinions, values, and outlooks on life are similar. After just one conversation, you feel as if you have known each other for a long time.

Over the course of time, your social interactions with this perfect customer may increase, as well as the quality of your business relationship. Your relationship may expand and deepen into a true friendship. Take a moment to consider what friendships you have developed over the years that began as business relationships either with customers or coworkers.

Conversely, it stands to reason that when you choose to follow another path, one that better suits another business, you find that the customers who come your way are not intended for you. They are less-than-perfect customers for you. Usually, this lack of fit becomes apparent immediately. Interactions with these customers tend to be confusing and unfulfilling. They want you to provide a product or service that you do not normally offer. Or they have no idea what they need and they want you to figure it out for them. They want you to make exceptions to your policies, to provide discounts, to provide credit terms beyond your standard agreements. Rather than adding to your business, they seem to take your time, your energy, and your resources. They take up space.

What they are actually looking for is another business to serve their needs. However, since you attracted them in the first place, this is a clue that some area of your business needs greater clarity. You may need to review your advertisements; perhaps you tried to compete by copying the strategy of another business instead of holding true to your unique mission. Or maybe you have been making exceptions to your policies for other clients and now you are getting a reputation that you don't want.

When a Perfect Fit Isn't So Perfect Anymore

The best time to collaborate with other businesses is when a previously perfect customer becomes a less-than-perfect customer for your business. How can this happen? Consider this example. Let's say that you are a hair stylist who owns a salon, and your specialty is cutting and styling hair. You don't do hair coloring because you are not good at it. You have a perfect client who, for years, has been coming to you to get her hair cut, and she is always happy with your service. Then she decides that she wants to color her hair. She has now become a less-than-perfect client, one you cannot satisfy with what you offer.

To pursue any less-than-perfect relationship would prove to be frustrating for both the client and for you. She doesn't want to be disloyal, but she wants her hair colored—and she wants it done right. You don't want to turn her down, but you don't have the level of training and skill required to do the kind of work she wants. So what do you and your client do? If you followed the common practice of businesses that will do anything to avoid having a customer go to the competition, you would try to continue to serve this client anyway, usually with disastrous results. However, the more strategic decision would be to consider it your responsibility to direct this less-than-perfect customer to a vendor who can provide a more perfect solution to your client's need.

This is also the most mutually satisfying way to be of service. In the case of the client who wants to color her hair, the most strategic solution is to create an *alliance* with another hair stylist, preferably one in the same salon for the convenience of your client, whose specialty is hair coloring. Together, you can both serve this client's needs so that she does not go to another salon.

In situations where it is not possible to serve all of a customer's needs within your own business, it's important to form alliances with others in your industry. For example, Sandi, a manager at an international car rental company, credits her success to referring her customers to other car rental companies whenever her inventory does not specifically meet her customers' needs. She recalls a time when a customer arrived at her counter with his family of five and their six suitcases. She immediately recognized that the full-size car they had reserved would not meet their needs for a stress-free vacation, but she didn't have any larger vehicles available for them to rent. Faced with this dilemma, Sandi arranged for the family to rent a minivan from another company. She recognized that what she was losing was only *the sale that day*—not the customer. And the goodwill she gained with this customer and with the other car rental company came back to her many times in additional reservations and referrals.

The Power of Two—or More

Over the years, we have developed working relationships with a large network of coaches, consultants, facilitators, trainers, and marketers in order to learn more about their most perfect clients. Knowing more about their missions and how they approach their work, we can better refer customers and clients to them. Although it may appear on the surface that we all do similar work for similar types of clients, we always find that our work is complementary, not competitive. That's because we see ourselves, our businesses, and our missions differently from other consultants. And our clients do, too.

Consider the following scenario that led to our business partnership. From clients and other consultants, we repeatedly heard about each other. It appeared that we were doing similar work. After first meeting through a mutual client, we agreed to meet again to discuss our personal missions and our services. At the conclusion of our meeting, we realized that most of our processes were separate and distinct. Jan's work was more focused on corporate strategic planning and sales team development, while Stacey worked in marketing and promotion. However, in a few areas our work overlapped: Stacey's clients would occasionally require corporate strategic planning, and Jan's clients would occasionally require marketing assistance. We had provided these occasional services ourselves because we didn't have any contacts we knew and trusted who did that type of work. By the end of our meeting, we knew that our personal and business missions were aligned. We decided to create a strategic alliance. Stacey referred her clients who needed the services where Jan was most effective, while Jan referred her clients to Stacey for her special skills. Through the success of these first attempts at collaboration, we saw that our work was most effective when packaged together, which is how we came to form our partnership.

The synchronicity of our missions quickly attracted the attention of a key executive of one of the largest telecommunications companies in the world. Interestingly enough, before our collaboration, each of us had wanted to work with this particular company and yet knew that individually we did not have all the resources required to meet the company's expectations. We had met this executive at a networking meeting. He was intrigued by the combination of skills that we had to offer and set an appointment to meet with us again. That one meeting developed into a perfect client-consultant relationship that would not have happened for either of us without our strategic alliance.

In some cases, creating strategic alliances allows businesses to serve different needs for the same clients. For example, if you are a divorce attorney, you may want to form alliances with attorneys in other specialties, such as estate planning or even criminal law, so that you can serve a larger number of potential clients together. You may also want to create alliances with accountants and family counselors, both of whom would know of marriages in trouble that may need your services.

Another form of collaboration occurs when you pay a referral fee to another professional who refers you a client who is not perfect for her but is perfect for you. And, of course, you can also receive a finder's fee when you refer a less-than-perfect client (for you) to another industry professional. In order for these types of referrals to be successful, it is essential that you take the time to determine the clients' needs so you can be sure you are matching them with the right collaborators.

Developing Collaborations That Work

Many of us have probably collaborated in the past and didn't realize it, perhaps because it is so easy to incorporate collaboration into our business practices. Yet collaborating *intentionally* is even more powerful.

How do you attract collaborators with whom you feel confident, trusting, and aligned? First, just as you create a Strategic Attraction Plan for your most perfect clients, you also create one for your most perfect collaborators. A good place to start is by listing the qualities that you want your collaborators to demonstrate. You might include qualities such as "an openness to collaborating," as well as "credible skills and knowledge," "integrity," "honesty," "commitment," and "focus," just to name a few.

The next step is to create alliances with those people who match your perfect collaborator profile. Begin by looking at your existing network of associates and the products or services they provide. In what ways can you mutually assist each other in serving your clients?

For example, if you are a software trainer and consultant, then you probably have relationships with computer hardware representatives, installers, networkers, and other software trainers and consultants. Take the time to learn what additional services each of these people offers that your clients might also need either now or in the future. Work together with these collaborative businesses to offer a free seminar for your most perfect customers on the latest technological developments. Your customers will appreciate the time and headaches that you save them by bringing solutions directly to them.

Beyond your existing contacts, many others in your industry are also potential collaborators. You can meet them by getting actively involved in industry associations and community activities that will increase your visibility, making it easier for like-minded people to find you. Contributing articles to trade publications serving your industry, accepting invitations to speak at industry forums, and taking the initiative to call on the owners of other businesses in your industry will also move this process along.

Once you have identified potentially perfect collaborators, it is important that all of you share openly with each other your definitions of a "perfect client." In this manner, you can clearly determine where your businesses overlap and where they are complementary. By including these professionals in your business growth plans, you are working to expand the pool of potential customers and potential revenue for all.

Pause for Reflection

Take a moment now to contemplate the following questions and write down your answers. These questions are designed to help you consider what might be possible for you and your business if you had at least one collaborator in your industry.

1. Who in your industry do you consider to be your main competition?

2. If you were not serving your customers, what other companies would be serving them?

3. What services do these companies offer that are the same as yours? Different from yours?

4. Have you ever referred one of your less-than-perfect customers to one of your competitors?

5. What would stop you from referring a less-than-perfect customer to one of your competitors?

6. Under what conditions would you refer a less-than-perfect customer to one of your competitors?

7. Do you belong to an association or organization dedicated solely to your industry?

8. If so, what benefits have you received as a result of your membership in that organization?

9. Who else do you know in your industry who belongs to this organization?

10. Can you name a less-than-perfect customer whom you would consider referring to a collaborator after reading this chapter?

If you want to make a dramatically impressive difference in your business, we invite you to meet or speak with a new potential collaborator every day for the next twenty-one days. You will create quite a stir within your industry, you will have a greater breadth of knowledge about your industry than other people providing similar services, and your reputation for being open and collaborative will spread very quickly, resulting in increased positive awareness and referrals. You may even have an experience similar to the one reported by George F. Phares, owner of Strategic Direction Resources:

My mission is to make lots of money and distribute it. . . . Recently, I received a call from a law firm I've worked with over the years. They had a client with a need for immediate help. Given my current client load, I would not have been able to give them the immediate attention they needed without reducing the level of services to existing clients. I provided the name of another consultant who might be in a better position to serve them. That was on Tuesday. As of Wednesday, I had appointments lined up for two new prospective clients whose time demands are not as immediate, making them more perfect clients than the one I gave up. When we distribute wealth (i.e., opportunities), it always comes back. Giving is receiving."[13]

Now we ask you, Whom will you call first?

5

Your Customers and Employees Want You to Succeed

> Imagine a seller/buyer relationship in which there is immediate trust and belief that the best solution will emerge because they are working together to discover a solution.
>
> *Sharon Drew Morgen*
> Selling with Integrity

DO YOU ever feel like you are running down a football field toward your goal and everyone—your customers, your employees, even your family—is playing for the other team? Do the people around you seem to be doing their best to block you and tackle you to keep you from getting into the end zone?

That is exactly how every day looked to Stacey before she began practicing the principles of Strategic Synchronicity. The faster she ran, the harder she fell.

She was telling a friend about her frustration with the latest tackle when the friend asked, "Stacey, what if you just *think* this person is playing for the opposite team? What if the truth is that he is really your teammate and he is trying to stop you from going the wrong direction down the field?"

This was the moment she was finally ready to receive the support and assistance from others that she desired but could never believe was actually possible to receive. Just as we discussed in chapter 2, the first step in attracting what you desire is to *envision* it and the second step is to be *open to receiving it.*

Imagine what it would be like if every one of your customers was actively supporting you and your business in your quest to succeed. Would they be providing referrals to other perfect customers? Would they be paying for the full value of your services? Would they be buying more often? Would they be placing larger orders? What would they be doing to help you that they are not doing now? What would they be continuing to do that they are already doing to help you?

Now that you have the vision of these new teammates assisting you to succeed, are you willing to receive their support? Being willing to receive their support implies that you are putting your full belief into your Strategic Attraction Plan. In order to believe in your plan, you must believe in yourself. Once that belief is in place, your business will never be the same. It's this confidence that causes you and your business to be much more attractive to perfect customers, employees, and vendors.

When you believe in yourself, the actions that follow will be completely different from those in the past. You will be likely to share information that you never considered sharing before. You will be likely to ask questions that you never thought to ask before. You will allow yourself the freedom not to know all the answers. You may even find that you don't have to work as hard. By trusting yourself and your Strategic Attraction Plan, you may find, as all of our clients do, that you can actually take a vacation and return to your office with everything running smoothly.

Say Good-Bye to Discounts and Special Offers

Let's begin with attracting perfect customers who support you in being successful. The only way to attract pure and altruistic customer loyalty and support is by being loyal and supportive of your customers. The usual surveys, free trial offers, frequent-flyer programs, and other incentives being touted by the proponents of "relationship" and "permission" marketing as the best ways to secure customer loyalty are no longer working. These premiums, techniques, and baits have simply trained consumers to wait for discounts and special offers before they buy. According to Geoffrey Brewer, writing in *Sales and Marketing Management* magazine, "One smart way to deliver value is to make sure that all your communications speak directly to customers' specific needs. The last thing customers want is more junk mail that bears their names but little else that is relevant to them."[14] The result of Brewer's research? Companies need to do a lot more listening in order to know what messages are the best fit for their customers' needs.

Remember, the third standard of Strategic Synchronicity is "like attracts like." If you want your customers to give their loyalty and support to you, then you must give it to them first. Solve a perfect customer's problem and you have gone far toward deepening your relationship.

Loyalties are formed through the building of mutually beneficial partnerships. As in any relationship, when there is an equal balance of giving and receiving, there is a natural desire to remain in association. One does not have to be coaxed, bribed, or prodded to maintain the connection.

Having interviewed a myriad of Fortune 500 firms and customer service experts, Rahul Jacob reports for *Fortune* magazine,

> The real magic of customer loyalty is . . . when you increase it, a beneficial flywheel kicks in. Powered by repeat sales and referrals, revenues and market share grow. Costs fall because you don't exert excess energy foraging to replace defectors. These steady customers are also easier to serve;

they understand your modus operandi and make fewer demands on employee time. Increased customer retention also
drives job satisfaction among your employees, in fact job
pride, which leads to higher retention. In turn, the knowledge employees acquire as they stay longer increases productivity. The very idea of customer satisfaction helps align
employees behind a common goal that everyone can understand.[15]

Let's take a moment to consider this concept closely. Think about
your favorite businesses. Perhaps there's a particular Web site where
you can find fascinating information quickly, or maybe your favorite
cleaner is the one that always seems to get the stains out of your silk
ties, or perhaps there's one department store at the mall where you
can always count on finding exactly the right item. Now think about
whom you interact with at those businesses. At the Web site, is it a
particular editor or customer service representative? At the dry
cleaner, is it the owner? At the department store, do you have a
favorite salesclerk? What do you know about these people? What do
you know about their interests, their likes and dislikes, their goals for
the future? What motivates them to get out of bed in the morning?

You probably know more than you think you do. You have picked
up a sense in your dealings with these people that they think like you,
have similar interests to yours, or sincerely care about you. You at
least know that one of their positive traits is that they make your life
easier. It's the reason that you keep coming back to these businesses.

Now consider whether all of your customers could say the same
about you. Have you shared both your personal and your professional
missions with them? Do your most perfect customers know that they
are your favorites? If they do, have you told them why they are so wonderful?

We are always amazed by the answers we receive to that last question. The vast majority of people say, "I told them I appreciate their business." Of course you appreciate their business. That almost goes without saying. What about telling them that you enjoy serving them because they always appreciate you, or they always have a funny story to share, or they always send interesting feedback about your Web site, or they always pay their bills on time so it makes it easy to pay yours on time, too? Share those specific details that will help these special customers realize that they stand out from the crowd.

What about your growth and expansion plans or the situations that have stopped you from achieving your plans? Have you shared them with your special customers and asked for their feedback? Did that last question shock you?

All too often, we realize too late just how much our best customers like us, depend on us, and want us to succeed. Think about how many times you have come to rely on a favorite hairdresser, restaurant, or other business only to be taken by surprise when you learned that it was relocating or going out of business because it was not as successful as it appeared. If you had known about the situation sooner, you would most likely have taken some action to help the business.

In the same way, your perfect clients don't want to have to find someone else to meet their needs if you go out of business. For them, it would be as if someone moved their lighthouse. Where will they find another guiding light? Where is their safe harbor in the middle of a storm? You must let them help you succeed by giving them the opportunity to provide input and advice along the way. This is where your willingness to trust the process is essential.

In part III, Tip 2, "You Are More Attractive When You Let Your Perfect Customers Know They Are Perfect," you will be guided in how to use this trust to develop a more loyal and supportive relationship with your most perfect customers. In the meantime, here are some other suggestions.

Ask, Ask, Ask, and Then Ask Again

Angela Caughlin of Millennium Success Consultants reports: "Recently, I was working with a large corporation that had used very few of the resources I had recommended. At our last meeting, I asked, 'What can we do to move this forward?' The person I was meeting with replied, 'I don't know,' but in the next breath he asked me if I could attend a meeting with one of his supervisors, one of the primary decision makers within this corporation. He had given me the answer I needed. This supervisor was the person that would ultimately move our business forward!"[16]

One of the most important pieces of advice that we have ever received about asking for feedback was given in a presentation by Jack Canfield, co-author of the Chicken Soup for the Soul books and products. He attributed the vast success of these products to his persistence in asking for what he and his business partner, Mark Victor Hansen, desired. They presented their idea for the first book to more than a hundred agents and publishers before they found one who was interested. Their commitment to their mission and vision is awe-inspiring.

How many of us ever apply that amount of persistence to obtaining feedback? Most of us would be concerned about "bothering" other people. Yet, as Jack says, what can it hurt to ask? Even if you are turned down, you are no worse off than you were before you asked. In the process of asking, you have the opportunity to receive valuable feedback that you would not have received otherwise. And there is always the possibility that your request will be accepted.[17]

Honestly Share Ourselves

We are always touched by the openness of the replies that we receive from readers of our "Daily Strategic Attraction Tip E-zine" (www.perfectcustomer.com) when we make a specific request for input. These readers, many of whom we have not met in person, freely share themselves and their advice with us. It is obvious that it is not too much trouble for them to take the time to help. In fact, they appreciate the opportunity to do so.

Take note that for Strategic Synchronicities to appear, we must be willing to give up our belief that it is not appropriate to bring our personal lives into our business lives. They are one and the same; their fragmentation is an illusion. It is important to combine our personal and business lives to create close, strong, and satisfying relationships with our customers.

By sharing our personal experiences openly, we can give others a truer sense of who we are. For example, we advocate being truthful with clients and customers when our personal lives interfere with our business, causing us to cancel an appointment. This honesty makes it easier for others to understand and to support us so that we can keep our agreements.

For example, Stacey travels to Chicago on a regular basis to help her father get back on his feet after he experienced a stroke. As you can imagine, our schedules went a little out of whack while she was first adjusting to stretching her capacity to take on additional responsibilities surrounding her father's care.

In addition, some new emotions began surfacing along with her new responsibilities. If she had attempted to keep those bottled up, they would have simply gotten in her way and made her completely ineffective in any area of her life, especially in the area of being of service to our clients.

Fortunately, she did not have to keep them bottled up. We are blessed with perfect clients and associates, so when she explained to our clients the reason she would have to be away from the office and why her replies to their requests might be delayed, they responded to her with genuine love and support. They also allowed her to express her true feelings of grief and concern so that she could more easily move through them. More than that, in welcoming the sharing of her authentic thoughts and feelings, these clients felt free to share their own trials and tribulations. Because of this mutual openness, the relationships we both have with these clients became stronger, more committed, and more supportive. This open sharing turned what could have been a tragedy into a triumph!

In moments of personal happiness, we are greeted with the same support from our perfect customers and collaborators. For example, when Jan's daughter and new grandson come to town, she arranges her schedule to spend quality time with them. By apprising her clients in advance and keeping them posted on her grandson's development, they can share in Jan's joy of being a grandparent. They also share the triumphs of their own children and grandchildren. This mutual sharing produces even richer relationships.

Perfect Employees Care, Too!

Although we have been stressing the importance of sharing ourselves with our customers, every one of the ideas in this chapter is directly applicable to our employees, our coworkers, and our vendors.

Our employees want to receive more than just a paycheck from their jobs. They want to feel that they are fulfilling their personal missions, too. More and more companies are devoting massive amounts of attention, time, and money to team building and other activities as a means of improving employee productivity and morale.

Yet it is still far too common to find that these same companies expect their employees to be excited and motivated by a company mission statement that does not give voice to the employees' personal commitments.

If you are a business owner, manager, or department head, consider whether you are aware of the personal and professional mission statements of each of your employees. If not, then consider sharing the core values exercise in chapter 1 with each of them so that you can assist them in aligning their statements with your company goals for the greatest success of everyone involved.

If you are an employee of a company, give your trust to your manager and share your personal and professional mission statements. Ask your manager to assist you in aligning these statements with the company's and department's goals for the greatest success of everyone involved. If you feel that this suggestion is naive and simplistic with regard to your relationship with your boss, then you may first want to use the exercises in part II to create your plan for attracting a more perfect working environment, one that supports and encourages you in aligning your personal and professional goals. The right position that fits your needs exists somewhere. The question is whether or not you believe you deserve it.

A foundation of support is essential to ensuring the success of the Strategic Attraction Plans you will create shortly. A lighthouse can't stand strong and tall and unwavering unless it is anchored into a firm foundation and has been built with the most effective materials for withstanding the mightiest storms. Remember, it's important to give yourself every advantage in becoming as attractive as you can be.

6

Create an Atmosphere of Accomplishment

THE SIXTH standard of Strategic Synchronicity reminds us of the secret to keeping our powers of attraction fully alive. Throughout the ages and in every spiritual belief system, the universal law of gratitude has been reinforced as the key to attracting abundance and prosperity. Our own experiences have proven that the more we express our gratitude, the more powerful is our ability to attract and make manifest what we desire.

> Simplicity, order, harmony, beauty, and joy—all the other principles that can transform your life will not blossom and flourish without gratitude.
>
> *Sarah Ban Breathnach*
> Simple Abundance

When your personal and business missions are aligned and you are envisioning what you desire, attracting what is perfect for you to attract, referring to others what is more perfect for them than for you, and receiving the support of your customers, only one action remains to be taken, and that is to say "thank you."

Sharing Our Gratitude

Most of us were taught as children that saying "please" and "thank you" was a sign of having good manners. These words are much more than that. They help us keep our focus on what we desire. One helps us to make a request; the other acknowledges that our request has been answered.

Most of us are comfortable expressing our gratitude when someone has presented us with a gift, and we know how to congratulate and acknowledge others when they have accomplished a goal or an outstanding feat. How many of us, though, take the time to express appreciation and acknowledgment to others simply for being in our lives? How many of us acknowledge our coworkers for the difference they make by doing their jobs, day in and day out?

When Jan was vice president of sales for a telecommunications company, she learned the importance of acknowledging others and expressing gratitude to them, even when there did not seem to be anything to acknowledge. One constant issue that confronted her team was the long sales cycle in the business. A lot of phone calls, action steps, letters, appointments, proposals, and negotiation conversations seemed to be needed to close a sale. She could see the excitement of each salesperson diminishing as the cycle extended over several months. It was easy to feel as if nothing was ever going to happen, as if the team wasn't achieving any results.

In discussing this situation with her business coach, Jan was inspired to create an atmosphere of accomplishment. She implemented a monthly meeting just for giving acknowledgments and discussing accomplishments.

Each meeting always started out with a heavy feeling; most of the time Jan regretted ever arranging the meeting. The heaviness was not a resistance to attending, it was the burden that the salespeople carried when they were dissatisfied with their results, felt unrecognized by their teammates and/or management, and were disappointed with their own lack of accomplishments.

The purpose of the meeting was for each person to share his or her thoughts about what he or she did and did not accomplish during the month. Then each person was acknowledged by his or her fellow team members for something that was noteworthy. Most of the time, the acknowledgment was not for a sale. A typical acknowledgment might be "I would like to acknowledge how you always have a smile on your face and how you always keep the team laughing."

At the end of each two-hour meeting, the whole team, especially Jan, felt much lighter and happier. The members of the team had the opportunity to clear the air, restore their self-esteem, and regain what was lost during the long sales process. The benefits were more than worth the time and energy expended on the meetings.

The ultimate benefit for the company was that people kept playing the sales game, even when they didn't have the results they were expecting. In addition, they played longer and more effectively, and they didn't carry over the failures of the previous month into the next month.

Through this experience, Jan also realized that most people do not naturally know how to acknowledge themselves for their own work. She began to train her team members in acknowledging themselves and others. She also provided training in how to *receive* the gift of acknowledgment. By providing a structure in which they could learn this skill, she was contributing to their ability to motivate and appreciate themselves, which proved to be a key element in the success of her team.

Sarah Ban Breathnach, in her life-affirming book *Simple Abundance: A Daybook of Comfort and Joy*, encourages her readers to create a "gratitude journal" as a means of recording their thanks each day for the abundance that exists in their lives. She affirms the universal law: "The more you have and are grateful for, the more will be given you." She also shares the idea that "As the months pass and you fill your journal with blessings, an inner shift in your reality will occur. Soon you will be delighted to discover how content and hopeful you are feeling. As you focus on the abundance rather than on the lack in your life, you will be designing a wonderful new blueprint for the future. This sense of fulfillment is gratitude at work, transforming your dreams into reality." [18]

When Stacey writes in her journal, she uses the concept of "grateful for some/grateful for more," which allows her to acknowledge that what she has already received is sufficient and complete for her and that she is also thankful for what has not yet manifested—the ever-increasing abundance that is still on its way. For example, she may write, "I am grateful I have ten new perfect clients, and I am infinitely grateful that I will continue to attract an additional five perfect clients this month." She finds that this practice works like a magnet in attracting all of her desired goals into her life more quickly, easily, and effortlessly.

Wayne Dyer, again in his marvelous work *Manifest Your Destiny*, writes that "When we feel grateful and give thanks . . . we feel complete. The nature of gratitude helps dispel the idea that we do not have enough, that we will never have enough, and that we ourselves are not enough." [19]

We are proponents of the concept that we create our realities (what we experience) by our perceptions (what we sense and feel). Synchronicity Strategists know that to change our realities, all we have to do is change our perceptions, and we change our perceptions by expressing gratitude for what we have received instead of focusing on what we are lacking.

Synchronicity Strategists never feel as if they are lacking customers because they are always grateful for the ones that they have attracted and the ones that they are in the process of attracting. And that expression of gratitude continues to bring more and more perfect customers to their doors and Web sites.

Earning "Frequent-Flyer Miles"

One Synchronicity Strategist gave the term "frequent-flyer miles" to those extra rewards we receive as a bonus on our path toward our intended goals. For example, Stacey set out to correct an erroneous charge on her cellular phone bill and wound up reworking her payment plan so that she received a credit of more than $300.

We all receive these types of serendipitous bonuses, yet how often do we fully notice and appreciate them?

Terri Lewis, a senior sales representative with Corporate Express Imaging & Computer Graphics Supplies, unexpectedly earned frequent-flyer miles and immediately expressed her appreciation: "I recently received two unexpected checks . . . $55 from a company and also $1,000 from a friend who borrowed it from me over a year ago. I immediately called and acknowledged [my friend] for being a man of his word."[20]

Consider the last time that you received something special out of the blue—an unexpected refund, a referral, an invitation. Did you notice and acknowledge it? A gratitude journal is a perfect place to keep track of all the frequent-flyer miles you receive.

A Perfect Day

Synchronicity Strategists begin each day by looking at their Strategic Attraction Plans. This is how they envision what they desire and make their request to attract it into their lives. Synchronicity Strategists end each day by being grateful for the requests that were fulfilled—the number of perfect customers that have been served, the amount of sales received, the lines of credit received, and so on.

Along with the expression of gratitude comes an assessment of how well they accomplished their mission that day. Just as they count the money they receive and expend in the course of doing business each day, Synchronicity Strategists hold themselves accountable at the end of each day so they know where they will start from the next morning.

Merry Mount, a behavioral strategist with Life Management Consultants, expresses this concept beautifully:

The way I wake up joyous is to go to sleep at peace. Before I go to sleep each night, I review my day to see if there was anything about it I did not like. Did I say or do something that might have been rude or uncaring? I ask myself how it served me to be rude or uncaring. Usually the answer sounds something like this: "I was rude because I did not feel that person was paying enough attention to me." I make a vow to do something for myself the next day so that I would fulfill that need within me to have attention. If I could have done something to help someone else and did not, I assess my actions to see if I am giving enough. After this exercise, I plan my tomorrow to make sure I correct anything I felt was out of balance. Right before I go to sleep, I find at least ten things for which to thank the universe. I get a perfect night's sleep because I have resolved all my conflicts. When I begin my morning meditation, I have no negative thoughts from the day before and can have a deeper and richer meditation. When I can thank God for my perfect day, he gives me another one.[21]

As you begin the Strategic Attraction Planning Process, keep the six standards of Strategic Synchronicity in mind:

- Be on purpose with your mission
- You have the power to attract whatever you desire
- Like attracts like: whom do you like?
- Choose collaboration, not competition
- Your customers want you to succeed
- Create an atmospere of accomplishment

Stop for a moment here and consider your day so far. Have you had the opportunity to accomplish your mission yet? What worked well in your day? What has not gone so well? For what are you grateful for receiving today? What goals are still to be fulfilled?

PART II

The Strategic Attraction Planning Process

YOU ARE now ready to *envision, create,* and *implement* your own Strategic Attraction Plan—a plan for attracting more of your perfect customers or clients. Before we begin, it is important to note that a Strategic Attraction Plan is distinct from a business plan, and both are necessary for the effective and successful development of any organization. A Strategic Attraction Plan is created to ensure that an organization is bringing the right customers to its door and Web site. A business plan makes sure that the operations of an organization will perfectly support these customers once they arrive.

> Visioning—constant interaction with the brightness of the future.
>
> *Jack Canfield*

The creation of a Strategic Attraction Plan begins with envisioning. This process is similar to the common practice among athletes of first envisioning themselves winning a race, a tournament, a game and then creating their training program to fulfill that vision.

It is also the same process that a lighthouse builder goes through when constructing the perfect structure on the perfect spot on the beach. The builder envisions all the possible scenarios—where, how, and when boats will need to depend on the lighthouse—and then builds the structure to accommodate those needs.

You are about to build your lighthouse. Each of the first four chapters in part II is written to guide you through one of the four steps of the Strategic Attraction Planning Process. The fifth chapter provides guidance for situations where different plans are needed for different stakeholders. In each step, by answering the main question of the chapter, you will design a particular aspect of your "most perfect customers" model.

- Step 1: What qualities do I want my perfect customers to possess and demonstrate?
- Step 2: What makes my perfect customers tick?
- Step 3: What do I want my perfect customers to expect me to deliver or provide?
- Step 4: What do I need to improve to attract or maintain my customer relationships with perfect customers?

To arrive at the answer for each overarching question, you will actually answer a series of questions within each chapter. These are the same questions that you ask yourself repeatedly—probably dozens of times a day. The goal for asking them here is to get the questions out of your head and the answers into the light of day, where they can be of the greatest use to you and your business.

You may find that you would enjoy doing these exercises with a partner or partners—perhaps a coworker or your entire team—for a richer experience. Whether you work alone or in a group, we recommend that you allow yourself two hours of uninterrupted time to create your first Strategic Attraction Plan. To create the plan, you will need one 8½-by-11-inch unlined white sheet of paper, folded in half lengthwise, with each of the panels labeled "Side #1," "Side #2," and so on. You'll also need a pencil, a quiet space, and a willingness to transform your business easily and effortlessly.

Let's begin.

7

What Is Your Vision of Your Most Perfect Customers?

> By asking for the impossible
> we obtain the best possible.
>
> *Italian proverb*

HOW WOULD you know if you attracted a perfect customer? As we have explored previously, the way to recognize a perfect customer is to first design a prototype of what your perfect customers would look like: how they would behave, what qualities and talents they would possess, what products and services they would purchase from you, what amount of money they would pay you, and how often they would need or purchase your products or services or visit your Web site.

Notice the "perfect client" qualities identified in the following passage shared by Michael O'Neal of People-Centered Training as he examines the difference between two clients for whom he performed the same services:

> I recently completed delivering a training program for a client that is a large consulting organization. I did well at this training, but I wasn't comfortable with the "energy," the stress/adrenaline level, and the "fun" level of the company. It just didn't "click." I decided that they are a good customer,

but not a perfect one. Shortly after that experience, I began delivering a four-week training program for another consulting company. As soon as I started, things were sailing so smoothly, the "clicks" and synchronicities just kept coming. They truly saw and highly valued my passion for what I do and gave me the positive feedback and support that are also important to me, and my best skills and "goldenness" were most important and valued by them! Our values are totally in sync, our life balance goals are in sync, and our focus on having fun while working hard are totally in sync . . . and I've found that these synchronicities make a huge difference in making a perfect customer for me![22]

Envision the Perfect Customer

Now it's your turn to create your own perfect client or customer profile. Rather than begin by making a list of the qualities and details you think you want to have in a perfect client or customer, you will begin with a visioning process. As you continue to read, please follow the instructions provided for conducting this process.

First, sit with your feet flat on the floor and uncross your arms and your legs. You will want to be completely open to receive the answers to the questions that we will be asking you shortly. It is so important your body remains uncrossed throughout the process that we will remind you to check yourself periodically.

Next, take three deep, long, slow breaths. Each time you blow out, allow your mind to relax. It's best to be completely relaxed as you begin your visioning process.

In your mind's eye, imagine yourself in your perfect work environment. Take a minute now and design the most perfect working space you can imagine. You get to create it, decorate it, furnish it however you wish. It is your space. And it is the space in which you will be working throughout this process.

As you create this space in your mind, answer these questions:

- How is it furnished?
- What color are the walls, floor, and furniture?
- Where is the space located?
- What do you see when you look through the windows?

To fully experience the sensation of being in, moving around, and working in this imaginary space, close your eyes and envision yourself in this perfect environment.

Now imagine that you are sitting comfortably in this perfect working space. Allow your mind to think back across the years and remember all of the customers you have served in every job you have held throughout your business career. Be sure to allow yourself to remember all of them—the good, the great, the not so great, the less than perfect, and the perfect. If you have been working for a number of years, you may have served hundreds, if not thousands, of people. Do your best to remember as many of them as you possibly can. Give yourself at least one full minute to let these people come back into your memory.

You'll probably notice a door that leads to the outside. Walk over to the door. As you are walking to the door, you will hear the sound of people talking on the other side of the door. These are all the customers you just remembered. Open the door and let each one of them come into your working space. If your space is a bit crowded, that is okay. These people will not be here for very long.

As they are entering your space, notice the expressions on their faces. Are they curious? Do they look friendly or unfriendly? Are they happy to see you? Are you happy to see them?

You may have a job position where you do not meet your customers face-to-face. Perhaps you serve them over the phone or via e-mail. If this is the case, then imagine what these customers would look like if you did meet them in person.

Once the customers are all assembled in your space, select the one who you feel is the closest to representing a perfect client or customer for you. In other words, the quality of the interactions that you have with this customer is as close to perfect as you have ever experienced. For example, this customer may always treat you with respect, pay full price, or refer other customers to you.

You may have many perfect customers. In that case, simply select one that represents all the rest.

On the other hand, you may not have even one perfect customer. If this is the case, simply select the one customer who comes the closest to being perfect. Or you may choose as a model of a perfect customer someone whom you would like to have as a client or customer. Consider why this person or company would be perfect for you to serve.

Take a moment now to ensure that your legs, arms, and hands are still uncrossed, and then make your selection.

Once you have made your selection, you may let all the others go. Thank them for the role they played in assisting you to create a Strategic Attraction Plan, escort them to the door, and then lock the door behind them. They have served their purpose, and you will not be needing them anymore for this exercise.

Again in your mind's eye, ask your perfect customer to have a seat and then sit facing him or her. Look closely at him or her. How would you describe the way the person is dressed? How would you describe the person's expression?

Think back to when you first met this person. Where were you? What was the year? Did someone else introduce or refer you? If so, who was that person?

Consider all of the interactions you have had with this person. What have you enjoyed most about serving this person? How does this person treat you?

Based upon the answers to these questions, how would you describe this person? Why do you enjoy serving this customer so much?

What are the positive qualities, characteristics, attributes, and talents of this person? For example, you may appreciate the fact that this customer

- always says "thank you" after every transaction
- always returns your phone calls within twenty-four hours
- places the largest orders of all of your customers
- always has a smile for you
- is always on time for appointments
- books an appointment every week
- refers other people to your store or Web site
- has a sense of humor

Give yourself sufficient time to think about this person and all the reasons that you enjoy serving him or her. Feel free to close your eyes to fully imagine this person before proceeding with this exercise.

Now, please turn to Side #1 of your sheet of paper, and follow these steps.

1. At the top of Side #1, write the title "My Perfect Customer Is [fill in the name of the person, if you know it]."

2. Under this title, list all of the positive qualities, characteristics, attributes, and talents of this person. Give yourself at least five minutes to make a complete list. If you do not know this person well, then write down at least five qualities that you would want him or her to possess. Be sure to write *only on Side #1* of your sheet of paper.

3. Review what you have written. Did you forget any positive qualities? If so, add them all to the list.

4. Put down your pencil. Ensure that your legs, arms, and hands are uncrossed.

5. Ask yourself, "Is there anything about this person that I would change to make him or her more perfect. If so, what would it be?" Perhaps you would like him to visit your Web site more often, or you would like her to spend a larger amount of money on your products or services, or you would like him to refer his friends to you. How could this person be an even more perfect client or customer? As the quote at the beginning of this chapter states, "By asking for the impossible we obtain the best possible." In other words, go ahead—ask for the impossible. What could it hurt?

6. Pick up your pencil and add to your list the additional positive qualities you just thought of. Again, be sure to write only on Side #1 on your sheet of paper. If you run out of room on this side, then use an additional sheet of paper to continue your list.

7. When you feel your list is complete, you may wish to review the list of qualities that we have compiled about our perfect clients (see the sidebar). Feel free to add any of these qualities and characteristics to your own list.

8. Take a deep breath. Be sure your feet are flat on the floor and your legs, arms, and hands are uncrossed. Allow your mind to be perfectly still so that the answer to the following question can come into your consciousness. It will take a few seconds for the answer to appear.

The question is, What is the perfect number of perfect customers for my business or company to serve during the coming year?

The Qualities, Attributes, and Characteristics of PerfectCustomers Unlimited's Perfect Clients

They want to attract only perfect customers, employees, and other stakeholders.

They keep their appointments.

They trust that we have their best interests at heart.

They come from a spiritual base.

They are decision makers for a growing, thriving business.

They are happy and share their good humor.

They are intelligent and demonstrate good common sense.

They have a strong network of friends and associates to whom they refer us.

They have a financial cushion to pay us.

They pay on time and up front.

They pay our full fee.

They plan ahead.

They participate in two or more of our workshops a year.

They book us to facilitate a session for all of their employees each year.

They appreciate and take our advice.

They understand and demonstrate that they deserve to be successful.

They know their business and personal missions are aligned.

They make a request to become our client.

They value our time.

They value their time.

They serve the needs of the community; they make a contribution to the community.

They enjoy paying us.

They provide us with repeat business.

They are peaceful, calm, and kind.

They want us to be successful and make a profit.

They and their employees subscribe to our on-line daily e-zine.

They possess and demonstrate mental and physical well-being.

The Qualities, Attributes, and Characteristics of
PerfectCustomers Unlimited's Perfect Clients, *continued*

They have offices in great locations around the world.

They always say "thank you."

They demonstrate integrity, loyalty, and honesty consistently.

They have realistic expectations of what can be achieved and when.

They want us to work only from 8:30 A.M. to 5:00 P.M. Monday
through Thursday.

They are decisive.

They want to personally guarantee their contractual agreements with us.

They provide us with five referrals each to perfect clients over a
six-month period.

They have clarity and focus.

They are collaborative.

They treat everyone like they are special.

They are sincere.

They have the same value system and work ethic as we do.

They are open-minded.

They are reliable.

They are true to themselves.

They praise us to anyone and everyone.

They are heart-centered.

They encourage us.

They are learners.

They challenge us to expand our capacities.

They visit our Web site once a day.

If you have the answer, write the number of customers at the bottom of Side #1. If not, take another breath, ask the question again, and then write the first answer that comes to you at the bottom of Side #1. The purpose for writing this number down is to provide a benchmark for reference as your plan grows and develops.

Can My Company Have More Than One Type of Perfect Customer?

You may be asking yourself what to do if you have more than one type of perfect customer. Perhaps your company sells different product lines and each one is designed for a different group of customers. You can use the same process again and again to create different Strategic Attraction Plans for each type of perfect customer you want to attract. You will find that many of the qualities of a perfect customer remain the same, while others differ from plan to plan.

We recommend that you continue with your first plan through the completion of Side #4. Then you can come back to this step and begin to create a plan for a second type of perfect customer.

Before we proceed to Side #2, we would like to share a tip with you. Be sure to keep this list of qualities near you throughout the day. Look for perfect qualities in every man or woman you encounter, then add those qualities to your list. Television, magazines, radio— these are also resources for finding the qualities that you want to have in the people who surround you every day. Whether you already have a good idea of what you want or your vision is still a bit hazy at this point, look to your world to find *specific* qualities to list. The more specific you are, the more *quickly* your perfect customers will appear.

8

What Makes Your Perfect Customers Tick?

THIS IS the most important chapter in this book. This chapter will guide you and your business through a paradigm shift that may seem so subtle, you will hardly know that anything has changed. Yet your relationships with your customers

> Life is either a daring adventure or nothing. To keep our faces toward change and behave like free spirits in the presence of fate is strength undefeatable.
>
> *Helen Keller*

will be profoundly different once you have undertaken this exercise.

In the previous chapter, you reviewed all the information you have collected through the years about the qualities that define a perfect customer for you and your business. Almost every item that you wrote on your list has probably been running through your mind on a daily basis. The last exercise was designed to get these ideas on paper to free up your mind for more creative thinking. Now you have the creative space in which to design your relationships with your customers based on something much more solid and fundamental than business alone.

The key to creating far more satisfying and synchronistic relationships is to say what usually goes unsaid in the context of business, to share the motivations and missions that drive us and our customers to get out of bed each morning and face another day. When we know what motivates our perfect customers—what is most important to them in their lives—we will be in a much better position to assist them to achieve their goals. We will also be able to relate to our customers as vibrant people who have as much at stake in the success of our business as we do. This is where Strategic Synchronicity starts.

At the top of Side #2 of your sheet of paper, write the title "What Makes My Perfect Customer Tick?" Now return to your perfect imaginary work space, where your perfect customer is still sitting and waiting for you. Ask your customer the following questions:

1. Why do you get out of bed in the morning?
2. Who is the most important person to you in the world?
3. What is most important to you in the world?
4. What do you want to achieve before you leave this world?
5. What do you really love about your life?

Write the answers you receive on Side #2 of your sheet of paper.

Did you find that you knew how your perfect customer would answer each of these questions? If the answer is yes, you are well on your way to building a strong and lasting relationship together.

If the answer is no, good! That means your foundation for a great relationship is ready to be set. This foundation can be created by asking the same questions of yourself. Based on the principle that "like attracts like," you can be assured that your most perfect customers are motivated by the same missions, issues, and challenges as you are.

Take a moment now and ask yourself the questions above and write down your answers.

You may find the answers provided by fellow Synchronicity Strategists to be of assistance in considering what motivates you.

Ed Young, president, Edwin G. Young II Insurance Agency, shares his thoughts:

> What makes me tick is to love and be loved by my family and friends (which includes my clients). I want to be excited about life and all the adventures of seeing new places and doing new things while also enjoying the revisiting of old familiar places. I want to make a difference in the lives of others by being of service to them in whatever realm that they need. I need and want to be spiritual and share my spirituality with whomever I come in contact. What *really* makes me tick is being the best that I can be with no apologies.[23]

Cynthia Cannizzaro, interior design and furniture director, provides this thoughtful response:

> What gets me out of bed is knowing I will see the two beautiful creatures God has entrusted to my care, their young smiles and the excitement of their new day and what they will do with it. Also, I love creating inspiring spaces that empower people; I feel it is a contribution to the world that my spaces make people feel more productive than ever before.[24]

Gary Young, president of Avela Corporation, is motivated by being a problem solver:

> What gets me out of bed is having the solution to a problem. I can't wait to get up and implement the solution. This is the best motivator. There is nothing greater than intellect creating from whole cloth. This is the ultimate in creativity and satisfaction.[25]

Productivity and achievement coach Linda Starr is motivated by a variety of factors. What gets her out of bed is the following:

1. Having adequate sleep; I feel rested and as if lying around in bed is a waste of time.

2. Having something compelling to work on: a new project, something that really excites me.

3. Feeling inspired by what the day has in store, seeing how the tasks are in alignment with my mission.

4. A sense of urgency and excitement, similar to being a child when you can't wait to get up and start playing![26]

Perhaps you are like Stacey, who reports that what gets her out of bed is being of service. Her morning habit is to wake up with enough time to look over her coming day and see where she can be of service. At a certain point in her review of the day's activities and the opportunities for service, no matter how tired she feels, she becomes so energized and joyful that she must jump out of bed and get to work!

Or your motivation may be similar to Jan's. One of her motivators for getting out of bed is knowing that her day includes causing the "lights to come on" for her perfect clients.

Before proceeding to the next chapter, be sure to write down at least one of your motivators.

9

What Do Your Perfect Customers Expect You to Deliver?

> What would you attempt
> to do if you knew
> you could not fail?
>
> *Robert Schuller*

NOW THAT you have a clearer picture of what a perfect customer or client is for you, it's time to turn your attention to what qualities and attributes make you a perfect vendor for your perfect customers. A relationship is a two-way street. If we expect our perfect customers to deliver all that we want, we must be prepared to deliver what they want, too.

How do you know what your customer expects of you? The answer is simple. As with every other part of your Strategic Attraction Plan, *you get to say* what you want them to expect of you.

Does this sound impossible? Think of it as an affirmation and a reminder that each of us, through our business, is fulfilling our own unique mission. You are the only one who can create your business in the way that you do. This is just as true for the owner and board members of the business as it is for each of its employees.

To be your most attractive to perfect customers, you must be completely fulfilled through your work. The way to be completely fulfilled is to decide what you want to personally deliver and how you want to provide it to your customers, how you want to utilize your unique strengths, and how you want to express and act on your intentions and desires through your business and your position.

Take a moment to recall an experience you have had of serving both a perfect customer and a difficult customer. Do you agree that the only difference between these two types of customers is that one appreciated the way you do business and the other one would have preferred for you to do business some other way?

Both of these customers had certain expectations of what you would deliver or provide to them before they began doing business with you. In one case, what you wanted to provide and what the customer expected to receive were exactly the same. In the case of the difficult customer, his or her expectations were different from what you wanted and intended to provide.

Your perfect customers want what you want to provide. You don't have to wonder anymore if you are providing what they want. What you want to provide will always be a perfect match for the *perfect* customers' expectations.

Your responsibility is to become clear about *what you want to provide.* The following exercise will help.

Begin by putting your feet flat on the floor and making sure your legs, arms, and hands are uncrossed so that you are completely open to the possibility of a business that equally serves you and your perfect customers.

Write at the top of Side #3, "I Choose for My Perfect Customers to Expect Me to . . ."

Under this title, you will list all the services, products, and other items that you have decided your customers can rely on you to provide. Consider every detail that is important to you including, but not limited to, your pricing, your location, your advertising methods, the size of your staff, and so on. Most importantly, remember that you are listing *only* what *you choose and want* to provide.

For example, we choose to return phone calls within twenty-four hours. A client that expects that we will return phone calls within twenty-four hours will be quite satisfied with that service and is a perfect client for us. However, a client who expects a phone call to be returned within two hours will be disappointed and is not the perfect client for our business.

We could choose to adjust our company and our way of doing business to satisfy the less-than-perfect client. Once we do, though, we no longer have a business that satisfies us. Instead, based on our shared mission for our business, we choose to create the expectations that we want to fulfill, trusting that our clarity will attract more perfect customers and leaving no room for serving those who are less than perfect.

If you are concerned that by being "too picky" you will limit the number of perfect customers you could attract, don't worry. As we have mentioned previously, the clearer you become about what you want your most perfect customers to expect from you, the more of them will appear—quickly and easily.

Monk Simons of M2 Associates had this experience within one week of creating his Strategic Attraction Plan: "I wrote on my list that I wanted my perfect clients to expect me to be known as 'the marketing guy,' and 'that they trust that I will get the job done.' Within one week, I had four different companies approach me (unsolicited) to work for them. I am finalizing plans with the two that are the most perfect fit for me. I continue to update my Strategic Attraction Plan, and each time, new shifts occur within my business."[27]

It's now your turn to choose what you want to provide. As you create your list, remember to be as specific as possible about each item. If you have trouble getting started, you may wish to refer to the sidebar for suggestions.

Perfect Customers' Expectations

I choose for my perfect customers to expect me to

- provide the lowest prices. (*What does "lowest" mean?*)
- have a business that makes a profit. (*How much profit?*)
- have a Web site for my business. (*What information would the Web site contain?*)
- treat them with courtesy. (*What does courtesy look like?*)
- return their phone calls within an acceptable period of time. (*What is an acceptable period of time?*)
- act professionally. (*What does acting professionally look like?*)
- be an expert in my field. (*How do experts distinguish themselves from other people?*)
- have a receptionist take messages for me when I am out of the office. (*How do you want messages handled when the receptionist is out of the office?*)
- be referred to them by someone they trust. (*Would this be a friend, a family member, a coworker, or someone else?*)
- be in communication on a regular basis. (*How often is "regular" communication? What do they want you to communicate?*)
- be available when they need me. (*What if they need you at 2:00 on Saturday afternoon while you are at your daughter's soccer game?*)

This list should be at least as long as the list of perfect customer qualities you created on Side #1. When you have completed your list, read each item aloud to yourself. After each one, ask yourself, "Do I really choose to provide this service?"

For example, you may have written "I choose for my customers to expect me to be available when they need me." Now ask yourself, "Do I really choose to provide this service?" If the answer is "Yes, as long as they only expect me to be available Monday through Friday between the hours of 8:00 A.M. and 5:00 P.M.," add these new details to your list.

Do this for each item you have listed. When you have completed reviewing your list, you are ready for the fourth and final step of the Strategic Attraction Planning Process.

10

Where Do You Have Room for Improvement?

WHAT DO you have to improve to attract more perfect customers? The answer is simple: only those items that your perfect customers expect you to deliver. A more difficult question is, What are you currently working to improve that your perfect customers do not expect or want you to improve?

This is the most enjoyable stage of the Strategic Attraction Planning Process because it gives you the opportunity to both acknowledge your strengths and to identify where you can "turn up the power" in order to be even more attractive to a larger number of more perfect customers. This stage also prevents you from going in the *wrong direction*.

Often, one of us will come up with what appear to be visionary and creative ideas for improving our company. In the moment, they seem to be the key to achieving monumental growth. Daily, we compare these ideas with the list of what we choose to have our perfect customers expect us to deliver. Sometimes our ideas are completely in sync with our plan. Most of the time, however, these ideas would waste our time, money, and energy if we acted upon them.

Perhaps you, too, have headed down a path of improvement only to find out it was just a dead end. Here is an exercise that you can use to keep your company on track to your goals.

1. Turn to Side #3 of your Strategic Attraction Plan, entitled "I Choose for My Perfect Customers to Expect Me to . . ."

2. As you read each item on the list, determine if you and/or others in your company are able to provide the particular service or meet the expectation completely and fully right now.

    For example, if the first item on your list is "treat customers with courtesy," you would ask yourself, "Do we treat our perfect customers with courtesy 100 percent of the time—yes or no?"

    (Here's a tip: in answering this question, your first answer is the right one. If you have to think about the answer, then the answer is probably no.)

3. If the answer is no, circle the item and then move to the next item on your list. If you treat your perfect customers with courtesy only 98 percent of the time, that item should be circled.

4. If the answer is yes, move on to the next item on your list.

5. Repeat the question for each item on the list. Circle every item that you and your company are not able to provide or meet 100 percent of the time right now.

    Most of us are our own worst critics. This is why *it is important to get a second opinion.* Fortunately, you have a wonderful resource waiting for you back in the perfect work space in your mind.

    Before you return to that perfect work space, please be sure that your feet are flat on the floor and your legs, arms, and hands are completely uncrossed. Now, take a deep breath and slowly return to that perfect space in your mind. You will find your perfect customer still waiting patiently for you there. Take a seat across from your customer so that you may look into his or her eyes.

When you are ready, begin reading the list of expectations from Side #3. Read both the circled items and the noncircled items. Imagine that you are reading this list of expectations aloud to your customer. After each item, stop and ask, "Is this what you expect of me and my company?"

You may feel a bit silly doing this exercise. Yet if you consider what your perfect customer would say about each item, we promise you that you will be amazed at how much more detailed your list will become. You may even find that you have been too hard on yourself. You probably do not have to work nearly as hard as you initially thought to please your most perfect customer.

When you have completed this exercise, mentally thank your customer for the service he or she has provided to you in the creation of your Strategic Attraction Plan. Then, come back to your plan.

6. At the top of Side #4, write the title "What Do I Have to Improve to Attract More Perfect Customers?" Under this title, make a list of all the items that you circled on Side #3. In other words, the items that you circled on Side #3 will now be *written again* on Side #4.

7. Next to each item on Side #4, write the date by when you will begin to work on improving that item. Note that you should write the date when you will *begin* to work on improving this item, not when you will *complete* working on this item.

This list of improvements is not a "goals" list. It is your *strategic plan* for becoming more attractive to a greater number of perfect customers.

At this moment, you may not know how you are going to improve these items. All you do know is that you want to improve them.

How long do you want to wait before declaring that these are the services and expectations that you are committed to delivering so that you can be more attractive? Our recommendation is that you put today's date next to each one as your declaration that this is the day you are turning your attention toward improving each item on your list. Remember, where you put your attention is where your energy goes. Where energy goes, ideas follow. Just by giving these items your attention, you'll find that ideas on how to improve them will come to you in the perfect time and the perfect way.

With your declaration comes the commitment to building a stronger structure for servicing an ever-growing number of perfect customers who are now heading toward your light. Think of this structure as a body. In order for a human body to thrive, all the various elements—the limbs, the muscles, the organs, the cells—have to be fully developed.

Each element of the body matures at a different pace—it takes time for all of the elements to catch up with each other. It is much like a baby learning to walk. A baby's mind is able to conceive that it is possible to walk long before the muscles in the baby's legs are completely developed and strengthened so that they can support the baby in walking. The mind's knowledge helps the baby to persevere through the process of learning to walk. Without this knowledge, the baby would give up the first time he or she fell down. In much the same way, it is our responsibility and duty to hold the vision of our perfect business until all the elements of the business have developed the capacity to support the entire structure.

Ask yourself, "Do I choose to have my perfect customers expect me to hold the vision of my perfect business?" Of course, the answer is yes. So please add this expectation to your list on Side #3.

Here's a tricky question: Can you honestly say that you hold the vision of your perfect business 100 percent of the time? If not, then circle this item on Side #3, and then also write it again on Side #4. (If you think that you are holding the vision 100 percent of the time, please write it on Side #4 anyway. It can't hurt to declare that you are improving your commitment to holding your vision.)

Here is one more item to add to your lists on both Side #3 and Side #4: "I choose for my perfect customers to expect me to review all four sides of my Strategic Attraction Plan every day for five minutes."

This is the biggest improvement you can possibly make in your business. If you took no other action than to review your plan every morning, you would notice major shifts for the better in your company occurring very quickly.

Looking at your plan each day reconnects you with your vision. It will make you more magnetic, and it will provide you with the necessary perseverance and patience required while you are making all the other necessary improvements.

Can you imagine that it is possible to have the same experience of working in your business as Dan Krohn, attorney at law? He shares,

> After working with the Strategic Attraction Planning Process to identify my perfect client, I became convinced that there are indeed more than enough such perfect clients to keep me busy. The work started to flow in, and it's been coming in at an increasing rate ever since. What's more, I have the extraordinary pleasure of working exclusively with clients whom I like—a luxury few attorneys ever experience![28]

Robert Sgovio of Integrated Life Systems shared with us an experience that occurred for him shortly after creating his plan for the first time:

> I really loved the exercise of distinguishing the qualities and attributes of my "perfect customer." While reviewing my plan, I noticed that *all* of my clients had three things in common:
>
> 1. They are relatively healthy in body, mind, and spirit.
> 2. They all have abundant resources.
> 3. They are somehow using those resources to make a difference for humanity.
>
> In that moment, I clearly got my mission and niche market for the bodywork line of my business: to tune, empower, and support leaders who are creating projects that make a difference for humanity. Several of my clients are currently in the process of starting foundations that support global and local projects, such as assisting children in third-world countries and creating summer camps for disabled kids. These clients are leaders who feel they have a calling to use their resources to make a difference. My work empowers their health and well-being, supporting their ability to carry out their missions.[29]

If you would like to have an experience similar to Robert's, be sure that your Strategic Attraction Plan is located in a place where you can see it every day, first thing in the morning. Some of our clients keep their plans on their nightstands, others put their plans in their daily planners, and a few clever ones have put theirs on the bathroom mirror, where they can look at them while they are preparing themselves to be more attractive both inside and out each morning.

We ask you to note that, although your values stay constant, your visions can change. As the saying goes, "Be careful what you wish for; you just might get it." Once you do achieve what you think you desire, a whole new range of possibilities will open up for you and your company. You'll discover that your plans will continually change and bring forth deeper insights. To get to these deeper levels, just keep reviewing your Strategic Attraction Plan every day.

You may want to add one more area of improvement to your list: your readiness to accept what you desire when it actually shows up on the doorstep of your company. On Side #4, write, "I now *accept* [having a 10 percent increase in revenues, receiving five new perfect clients, receiving 5,000 additional hits on my Web site this week, attracting the perfect receptionist, that the perfect solution to my problem will appear today,] or whatever you desire."

How can something this simple, perhaps you would say even silly, be effective? When you access the power of the law of attraction, the result is produced simply and successfully—and synchronistically. As stated previously, the simplest way to access the power is through your own clarity of vision and your willingness to accept and receive the result.

That's where most people stop. So let's keep going!

11

Multiplicity: When One Plan Is Not Enough

> A good garden may have some weeds.
>
> *Thomas Fuller*

JUST AS a garden is more attractive when it is filled with a variety of plants and flowers, colors and hues, so too is your business when it is filled with a variety of perfect customers and other stakeholders, such as employees, vendors, partners, and associates.

When we are working to achieve truly big and great goals, such as attracting more perfect customers and clients, we are most likely not working on these goals by ourselves. We are working with partners or employees or investors or other stakeholders who are involved in helping us to achieve these goals. It is essential that these folks also be perfect for you in order for you to achieve your goals as quickly as possible with a minimum of distraction. Doug Upchurch, CEO of Insights-Austin, a global organizational change management corporation, reports,

> I created two new Strategic Attraction Plans—one to attract my "perfect consulting associates" and the other to attract my "perfect clients." Within three days, we had our first meeting with a large international company with headquarters

located here in Austin, Texas to introduce our Team Assessment System. Within 90 minutes, they committed to enroll two of their employees in our Team Assessment System accreditation program as the first step in training all of their U.S. employees in this System. They are also considering rolling out the training throughout their global operations. I left the meeting very excited and almost dumbfounded that it had all happened so quickly. I have experienced many quick sales since adopting the Strategic Attraction Planning Process, but this one took the cake.[30]

After creating your Strategic Attraction Plan over the last four chapters, you may now be aware that improvements are needed in your relationships with these other key stakeholders in order to meet the expectations of your most perfect customers and clients. If so, it is time to create a Strategic Attraction Plan for each group.

How is it possible to keep track of so many different stakeholders all at once? The answer is to make sure that you look at each plan every morning for five minutes to re-energize your powers of attraction. Then, trust that your plans are working throughout the day— and they always are.

This is the easiest, fastest, and most successful way that we have found to keep all of our relationships flowing in the same positive direction. And because these relationships are all flowing in the same direction, they easily move us forward over great distances in the shortest amount of time.

As we were creating our business partnership, we found that we had to overcome a basic way of operating we both shared—each of us felt that it was simply easier for us to do everything ourselves. We each had come to this conclusion based on prior experience. It had always seemed more difficult to get tasks done when other people were involved. It had also seemed that we had to compromise our goals in order to make everyone else happy.

This is a common problem. Two people enter into an agreement only to find that they have different expectations of how this agreement is to be fulfilled. Ultimately, the agreement is broken, feelings are hurt, and often the relationship is forever impaired.

This type of situation occurs when two parties enter into an agreement based on the assumption that they both have the same view and understanding of the agreement. Before any agreement is made, we must bring trust to the agreement—not trust of the other person but trust that whatever happens within the agreement is perfect for us both to learn from. Even if the agreement does not work out the way we think it should, we must trust that it is still perfect, and it is exactly what we need to be able to understand what we *do* want at that particular time.

One way to bring trust to the agreement is for both parties to create a "Strategic Attraction Partnership Plan" together to clearly spell out what each party desires from the other person. You can create a partnership plan with each of your employees, with your vendors, with your investors, and even with your spouse. This partnership plan will assist you in knowing immediately whether you have chosen a perfect partner because the agreement will not go further than the planning stage if the partner is not perfect. If the agreement is not meant to be, how will you know? Don't be surprised if you find that you are unable to keep your appointments to meet or the two of you are unable to come to an agreement on a key point.

If the two of you progress beyond the planning stage into a full agreement and *then* difficulties begin to appear, you can trust that you and your partner are being given a new opportunity to grow together. Take a look at what you now want to include in your agreement that you were not ready to accept previously.

Have you ever had the experience of entering agreements that have taken years to finalize? At first, they seemed to progress, and then all of a sudden, they stopped for a while either because your expectations were not met or you did not meet your partner's or your customer's expectations. Later, by "coincidence," you came back together again and picked up where you had left off. Can you now see that the delay was perfect—and that it was simply a delay, as opposed to a broken agreement—because you both needed that time to develop the skills that would allow you to meet each other's expectations?

In other cases, you may have entered negotiations that stopped and were never resumed. You now can see that you had come to understand that you were no longer interested in meeting the expectations of the other party, that you had become more clear about what worked for you and what did not. Again, this was a perfect situation because you could not have gained that understanding without having that experience.

Reflect on the various agreements and contracts that you have entered into with other people. Consider if those that are currently active are working the way you expected or if you are experiencing disappointment with your partner, coworker, employee, or vendor. If the latter is true, bring trust to the agreement by recognizing that this disappointment is giving you another opportunity to understand what you want from the agreement. Ask the other party to create with you a Strategic Attraction Partnership Plan so that each of you can become perfectly clear about your expectations of each other.

Can you see that a paradigm shift is occurring here?

While it may appear that the simplest and fastest way to accomplish our goals is to create only one plan for attracting perfect customers, the truth is that the fastest and most successful way to attract these customers is to create multiple plans for all the people that affect our lives and our businesses to ensure that all of these relationships are flowing in the same positive direction—toward the achievement of your goals.

Currently in our business, we have eight plans working at the same time to support us both in *attracting* and *maintaining* eight different groups of stakeholders:

1. Perfect clients for our workshops

2. Perfect clients for private facilitation and coaching

3. Perfect business partners and affiliates for expanding our business

4. Perfect clients for our train-the-trainer Synchroncity Leadership Program

5. Perfect meeting planners, speakers' bureaus, and talk show producers

6. Perfect vendors

7. Perfect publisher

8. Perfect spouse

Not only can you create a Strategic Attraction Plan for each stakeholder group, but you may also wish to create a different plan for attracting the most perfect customer for each of your company's products and services.

Here are two Synchronistic Perspectives from Synchronicity Strategists who have found the key to successful business agreements.

Ann Anders, vice president for sales and marketing for www.yoonite.net, shares this story:

First, I created Strategic Attraction Plans for my perfect mate, my perfect business partner, and my perfect client. Then, I asked my business partner, James, to create his own Strategic Attraction Plan of what he wanted in a perfect business partner. I believed this exercise took us to the next level in our commitment to each other and our business. . . .

Yet, in a short time James proved to be more talk and less action. . . . I decided that doing business with him was not meant to be. However, I now know that our relationship was a perfect fit because he introduced me to the person who is my "most perfect" business partner, Theresa. We met at a meeting that James coordinated. Having already given considerable thought to the characteristics of my perfect business partner, when she appeared I was ready to embrace her with ease.

Theresa and I instantly "clicked" and began having frequent conversations about her business idea to create an ISP/mall. In a short period of time, I realized I was aligned with her idea and accepted my most perfect position.

She is my perfect partner because she is creative, intuitive, and wants to give back to the community. She is a joy to be around, and it feels as though we have known each other for a very long time. She also has helped me to become clearer about additional qualities I enjoy having in a partner, such as strong family values, loyalty to family and business partners, and fairness in business dealings.[31]

Evalyn Shea, owner of Shea Writing Solutions, a technical writing company serving the oil and gas and technology industries, reports:

I found it interesting that just a few days after my office manager and I had created a new Strategic Attraction Plan for a more perfect receptionist, our current receptionist unexpectedly resigned. I know this was no accident. Although we dearly loved her, she was not a perfect fit for the position of receptionist, and we did not have another position for her. The relationship did not end, however, as she honored me by asking me to be her mentor. I continue to be an influence in her life, encouraging her to complete her education and fulfill her dream of becoming a lawyer. And I continue to be influenced by her overflowing laughter and joy in people and living. A perfect win-win situation.[32]

To assist you in manifesting Strategic Synchronicities like these, you will find twenty-one Strategic Attraction Tips in part III of this book. Each daily tip is designed as a companion to each of your Strategic Attraction Plans. Each one will take your plans to a deeper level.

Strategic Attraction in Action: Twenty-One Daily Tips

> Bad habits are easier
> to abandon today
> than tomorrow.
>
> *Yiddish proverb*

ACCORDING TO behavior therapists, it takes a human being at least three weeks to turn a new behavior into a habit. So here are twenty-one daily Strategic Attraction Tips—one for each of the next twenty-one days—to assist you with your transformation into a Synchronicity Strategist.

A *Synchronicity Strategist* is someone who is actively engaged in the daily practice of the Strategic Attraction Planning Process. Synchronicity Strategists always expect to receive perfect customers to serve in any given moment. Synchronicity Strategists instantly recognize the powerful spark of Strategic Synchronicity when they meet a perfect customer for the first time, and they continue to look at their Strategic Attraction Plan daily to ensure these Strategic Synchronicities occur on a regular basis. Their goal is building long and satisfying relationships with all of these customers.

Each of these twenty-one tips contains a Synchronistic Perspective (a quote from a Synchronicity Strategist), and a Strategic Synchronicity exercise. In addition, most of them include true vignettes of how the tip was successfully applied by other Synchronicity Strategists. You will find that the six standards of Strategic Synchronicity are also inherent in each of these twenty-one tips.

We recommend that you practice each tip in the order provided, from one to twenty-one, to move yourself and your business toward new heights of success and satisfaction. Your Strategic Attraction Plan is your road map for the journey, and these tips are your mile markers.

Each morning, as you ready yourself for your business day, prepare to embark on an important expedition—the one to your dreams. As with any other important trip, it is wise to consult a map to determine the most direct route to your destination so you can arrive in the shortest amount of time. This is why it is essential to take five minutes at the start of each day, before you begin conducting business, to review your plan.

When you neglect to consult the plan before starting your daily journey, you will find yourself running in circles, being surprised by detours, and winding up on dead-end streets. As a result, the journey will be much less fun and enjoyable, and you will tend to visit more rest stops than you had planned.

Think about it this way: Just as you must fill your gas tank before setting off on a long road trip, so must you re-energize yourself each morning in order to be as attractive as you can to as many potentially perfect customers as possible each day. The energy you need is accessed by tapping into your plan.

Each time you look at your plan, you will increase the speed at which you attract perfect clients and customers. Moving at such a high velocity may feel a bit uncomfortable at first. You may feel overwhelmed by the increase in business, and your natural tendency may be to step on the brakes to slow down the process. Here's a word of caution: Don't do it. If you do, you will find yourself right back at the starting line.

How will you know when you are stopping yourself in your tracks? Watch for these warning signs:

- You *stop* looking at your Strategic Attraction Plan for five minutes every morning. (*"Business is good, so I don't need to look at it anymore."*)

- You find yourself taking a detour from your path to deal with crises that seem to pop up from nowhere. (*"Wouldn't you know it—problems always pop up just when business is going well."*)

- You feel lost, scattered, unfocused, tired, less able to generate excitement and passion for your businesses. (*"I need some rest; I can't handle one more thing to do."*)

To ensure that you stay on your course, you must keep looking at your plan. You can trust it to contain the signposts to guide you in the right direction easily and effortlessly—and profitably.

Start your motor running.

Get ready. Get set. Go!

You Are More Attractive When You Focus on the Horizon

> The place where the sun isn't shining now will be illuminated in a few hours.
>
> *Sophia Bedford-Pierce*
> The Key to Life

WE ARE much more attractive when we lift our heads and set our eyes squarely on the horizon. That is where our vision lies, although it may take some time for our eyes to adjust and bring that vision clearly into focus. Most of the time, we are focused on what is two feet in front of us—the next phone call to make, the next crisis to handle, the next proposal to complete, the next meeting to attend.

How often during the day do we focus on the horizon? How often do we stop and share the beauty and glory of our private vista with someone else—an employee, a coworker, a client, a friend? Usually, we think that if we can just get "caught up" with the work on our desk, we will have time to think about the future. And there is always more work.

Today, view your Strategic Attraction Plan as a picture of the horizon, as the sun rising on your vision. This is why it so important to look at your plan every morning. It is your personal sunrise.

How wonderful would it be if the sun rose more than once a day? Looking at your plan throughout your day is as refreshing as a new sunrise. Your attention rises above the mundane matters of the day. Instead of being dragged down, you are inspired and filled with energy. You are reminded of your true mission and aspirations. You have given yourself a fresh start.

Business coach Joan Bolmer tells her story: "During the past two months I have been in pain and unable to do the most normal things, like sit in a chair for more than five minutes. The only thing I could do during my hours of pacing was to look at my Strategic Attraction Plan and talk to myself about my goals. Miraculously, this month is the best [moneymaking] month I have had since November of '99. Referrals have just shown up!"[33]

Patty Walters, a consultant for Shell Services International, is mastering her ability to look at multiple horizons: "I am keeping focused on the horizon much more often. I have created many attraction plans for various relationships, and I love looking at them daily. I feel cheated if I miss a day, so I believe that's a good sign that it is becoming part of who I am."[34]

Meanwhile, Carol Cooper, CPA and possibilities coach, has found a quick and effective way to stay in touch with her Strategic Attraction Plan. She places a note by every phone in her office, her home, and her car. On this note, she lists the short-term revenue goals, the long-term revenue goals, and one fun goal (like a two-week vacation to Tahiti) from her plan. She has been practicing this exercise for quite a while and is convinced that her success is directly tied to this exercise.[35]

What lies on your horizon? How many times a day will you focus on your own private sunrise?

You Are More Attractive When You Let Your Perfect Customers Know They Are Perfect

TODAY'S TIP reminds us of the synchronistic principle that marketing is simply building relationships. The most effective way to build stronger relation-

> It takes a lot of courage to show your dreams to someone else.
>
> *Erma Bombeck*

ships with your most perfect customers is to share with them the Strategic Attraction Plans for which they are the inspiration.

When you share your plans with your perfect customers, you are actually offering those customers a unique opportunity to provide their feedback and support. And that in turn engenders their loyalty.

"If you're serious about fostering loyalty," says Frederick Reichheld, author of *The Loyalty Effect*, "you find out how to deliver far better value to your most important accounts. The only strategy for sustained growth is high retention."[36]

In fact, a study by Bain & Company, a Boston-based consulting firm, confirmed that the average Fortune 500 company could instantly double its revenue-growth rate with a 5 percent increase in customer retention. A small to midsize company could double its profits in ten years simply by increasing its customer retention rate by 5 percent.[37]

Today, we encourage you to phone a perfect customer to let him or her know that you are expanding and improving your business. The primary purpose of this call is to invite this customer to an "honoring lunch" with the following intentions.

1. To share the list you created of perfect qualities and attributes that this customer demonstrates. This is the most important element of the luncheon. How many of us are ever honored in such a way? By sharing with your perfect customers the specific characteristics and qualities that you appreciate and honor about them, you will restore their spirits and give them an unexpected lift in their day. They will understand why their opinion is so important to you as you continue through the following steps.

2. To receive this customer's input on your lists of "What Makes My Perfect Customer Tick?" and "I Choose for My Perfect Customers to Expect Me to . . ." Does this customer agree with your lists? Does he or she have any additional ideas to add to your lists? Is this customer being served in the manner he or she wishes to be served? You might be pleasantly surprised to find that you have been expending extra energy in your business that you don't have to expend.

3. To thank this customer for his or her business. If it weren't for your perfect customers, you would probably not be in the business you are in.

4. To better understand this customer's plans and problems. When you assist customers in solving one of their problems and take an interest in what they want to accomplish in their lives and/or businesses, you've taken a step toward deepening your relationship. You stop being a vendor and become a partner!

If you are unable to meet in person, then simply call or e-mail one of your perfect customers today to schedule a phone appointment in which you can share your plan. Be sure to schedule at least thirty minutes for this phone call.

We guarantee that this exercise will result in a mutually fulfilling conversation that will open the door to an even better and more secure relationship. If you share your plan sincerely, from the heart, your perfect customers will be so grateful for the experience that they will most likely respond by asking how they can be of greater assistance to you.

We recommend that your response be "I only want to work with people just like you. Do you know of anyone that I would enjoy serving through my business?" Then ask for an introduction to those people.

Next, be sure to ask your perfect customers how you can be of greater support to them, and *thank them* for their generosity in helping you to grow your business.

Gem Smith, a freelance writer, took action by inviting a perfect *potential* customer to an honoring lunch. She says, "I met with a special event planner. In the course of our conversation, I learned that she could use help with her proposals and her competition entries. Another possibility down the road might be help with scripts. Before I left, I learned that she needs a better photographer. I am referring her to two."[38]

Suzanne Ellis also experienced the joy of hosting an honoring lunch: "I honored my perfect client yesterday—she welcomed the break from packing for a long trip and was delighted to visit her favorite coffee shop. Christine was moved by what I shared from my list of her perfect client qualities. She said it was delicious to be able to slowly take in and savor each bite of acknowledgment. Christine thought that I was absolutely on target with my list of items that I want my perfect client to expect me to provide, and she offered a few suggestions to enhance my plan. She is 100 percent in support of me and my vision."[39]

Consider what might be possible for you and your business if you were to invite one of your employees or a coworker to an honoring lunch. Could it be just as fulfilling as the one John Clark, a Farmers Insurance Group district manager, experienced? John reports, "My perfect agent was completely shocked that I had chosen him out of the hundreds of agents I had from which to choose. I began reading the characteristics that make him my perfect agent, and he was floored. After I finished, and he caught his breath, he shared with me how he desperately needed to hear this acknowledgment. I left our meeting feeling awesome."[40]

It's easy to imagine the ennobling difference that John made in his perfect agent's day as a result of taking the time to honor those perfect qualities.

Now, it's your turn. Who will you invite to an honoring lunch today? *Bon appétit!*

You Are More Attractive When You Understand That Customers Are Seeking You

> Learn to pause . . .
> or nothing worthwhile
> will catch up to you.
>
> *Doug King*

TODAY WE have an opportunity to experiment with the vision that our business is actually a lighthouse with the sole responsibility of shining its light in the midst of a dark and stormy night, directing boats at sea to a safe harbor. In other words, we are encouraging you to remember that *your customers are looking for you*, and they are counting on you to make it easy to find your business in the places where they are looking.

Stop for a moment now and consider how often you've said to yourself and others that you are "looking for" the perfect client, the perfect employees, or the perfect investor. The minute that you created your Strategic Attraction Plan, that statement was no longer true. What is true is that you are in the process of *attracting* your perfect clients, customers, employees, investors, and vendors.

It's so much harder to look for people. First, you do not know where to start looking. Second, you're not sure you'll know them when you find them. Third, you're not sure if they will let you do what you want to do for them when you find them.

Instead, it's much more preferable to stand still and get clearer and clearer about what you are in the process of attracting to you—much like a lighthouse. A lighthouse stands in the same spot, on the same shore, never leaving that spot through eons. Boat captains at sea know that the lighthouse will be in the same spot should a storm arise and they need to find a safe harbor. And when that storm arises, those captains count on the fact that the light from the lighthouse will get stronger and stronger, emanating from the same spot. They are *attracted* to the light, which allows them to see the way to a safe place.

To apply this principle to our marketing plans requires us to believe that *customers are seeking us.*

- They have needs to be met right now.
- They have goals to be achieved right now.
- They have a mission to be fulfilled right now.
- They are seeking the perfect collaborators to assist them in achieving all they desire right now.
- And they want to know where to find them—*fast!*

The question to ask yourself is, *"How can I help them find me faster?"*

Imagine that you are a strong and powerful beacon lighting the way through the fog. What is the quickest and most perfect path to your door?

The answer lies in knowing how your most perfect customers found you in the past. Take five minutes now to make a list of the different ways that your most perfect customers first found you or your company. Did you make a cold call to them? Did they receive a note or a mailing from you? Did they meet you at a networking event? Did they meet you through a friend or a business associate? Did your company advertise in the publications they read? Did they meet you at a conference? Was your Web site hyperlinked to related Web sites they were already visiting?

The way these perfect customers found your company is how you are meant to attract more of them. If you don't know how these customers found you, then it's time to call one or two or three of your perfect customers and ask them for their input on how they would want to find you if they were still searching for you.

For those of you who might be asking, "Isn't that a bit like putting all your eggs in the same basket?" the answer is yes!

It seems to be working well for Select Press, a California-based publishing company that grosses about $300,000 annually, with almost no expenses, by attracting and retaining a very "select" audience for each of its newsletters and journals. For each new publication he creates, owner Rick Crandall first identifies the most perfect readers and sends a personal invitation to each one to receive a subscription. He estimates that 90 percent of his business comes from repeat customers and their referrals.[41]

The process of strategic attraction involves developing quality relationships. The more focused your light, the brighter it shines. Conversely, when you scatter your time, energy, and money to participate in a variety of promotional activities in order to cover a broad area as quickly as possible, your light isn't much more than a flicker.

As you gather information from your most perfect customers, you will want to record their answers in your company's customer information database for future reference and tracking. The advent of such database systems makes it easy to remember our most perfect customers, to interact with them one at a time, and to identify similar likes and dislikes among this valuable group of customers. Maintaining your database is one more step on the path to building the lasting relationships that are the foundation of the strategic attraction process.

If you are ready to be a light in the darkness, here's a bonus tip for today. The next time you are asked, "What types of customers are you looking for?" respond with the following answer: "I am in the process of attracting [fill in the blank with one or two qualities from Side #1 of your Strategic Attraction Plan]." For example, "I am in the process of attracting five new customers this week that are the sales managers of Fortune 500 companies."

You will be amazed by the attention you receive simply by using this statement.

You Are More Attractive When You Make Irresistible Improvements

> When you're through changing,
> you're through.
>
> *Bruce Barton*

YOU ARE now on your fourth day as a Synchronicity Strategist. You are ready to move the process along at a faster rate by making irresistible improvements.

You and your business become more irresistible and attractive each time you attract another perfect customer. In order to make room for more of these, you have to release all of your less-than-desirable customers.

We are not asking you to "fire" your less-than-perfect customers. The truth is that without these customers paying the bills, you probably would not have a business at all. However, you must *stop complaining* about these clients. Instead, recognize that they have the ability to perform a perfect service for your business if you let them.

Problem customers are actually your best tools for strengthening your synchronicity muscles to attract a larger number of more perfect clients. How can that be? These less-than-desirable customers are in our lives and our businesses to show us where we have been settling for less than we deserve. *And they have a lot to teach us.*

Today, give yourself a half hour in which to complete the following exercise:

1. Take a few minutes to think about the less-than-perfect behaviors, attributes, and traits that each of your customers is demonstrating.

2. Make a written list of these less-than-perfect traits.

3. Next to each less-than-perfect trait, write down what would be the opposite, positive trait. For example, if one of your less-than-perfect customers is always late to appointments, then the opposite, positive trait would be "always punctual."

4. Transfer this list of positive qualities to your perfect customer profile (Side #1) of your Strategic Attraction Plan.

5. On a separate sheet of paper, write, "I now thank [name each customer who served as a role model for this exercise] for giving me this opportunity to become more clear about what is perfect for my business." Do not show this piece of paper to anyone else. It is for your eyes only.

6. *Be prepared* for one of the following two possibilities to occur in relation to your less-than-perfect customers:

    a. Over a relatively short period of time, the behavior of those customers will automatically and dramatically improve. You will find that they actually become more perfect for your business.

    b. They will simply stop doing business with you and will drift away without a conflict.

    If the second possibility occurs, *do not panic.* You can trust that it means they are clearing the space for more perfect customers to come into your business.

TIP 5

You Are More Attractive When You Listen to Your Little Inner Voice

> Intuition can help you find the information you need, both about yourself as well as your market, to make a difference and profit by being yourself.
>
> *Laura Day*
> Practical Intuition for Success

STACEY TELLS the story of driving past the office of one of her clients, a customer service manager of a bank, and hearing a little voice in her ear telling her to stop and say hello to her customer. Although she didn't have an appointment, she listened to the voice and dropped in unannounced. Her client was happy to see her since she was just finishing a meeting with one of her perfect customers. The synchronicity of the timing of Stacey's unplanned visit did not escape her as her client introduced her to the customer and praised Stacey's workshop. The client was so enthusiastic and complimentary that the customer registered for the next workshop.

This is what it's like to attract perfect customers easily and effortlessly. Can you remember the last time that you had such an experience?

Today's tip is to consider that you are more attractive when you are listening to your little inner voice.

Can you tell the difference between your inner voice and your mind? Jan finds that her mind acts like a director barking out orders as to what to do next, while her inner voice more gently guides her to the right path.

Nicole Smart-Wycislo, president of Verb Consulting, further elaborates, "Being in tune with our voice is being connected with God, plain and simple. When my Voice inside my head speaks, I know it's God talking to me. How I distinguish the Voice from my ego is that the Voice is 'dead on and never wrong'—I feel the connection to the Truth down to my bones."[42]

When your little voice prompts a call or a visit to a particular customer and you act immediately, you will find that you have the strongest ability to attract what you want into your business. Patricia Rumble, massage therapist and Reikimaster, says, "The other morning I couldn't decide whether to attend a chamber of commerce meeting on 'Shameless Self-Promotion.' My 'muse' said, 'Get yourself up and go to that breakfast.' So I went and I took brochures, business cards, and a sheet of paper with a list of six examples of clients who had benefited from my work. . . . I got two clients from that abbreviated talk and perhaps more."[43]

Of course, if we are being honest, most of us would admit that we often hear the voice yet fail to act on its advice immediately. We may file away the idea or put it on our to-do list. Something else usually seems more important at the time. But if we don't act upon the idea at that very moment, we lose it, we forget about it.

When your inner voice last spoke to you, what did it say? Did you let it guide you, or did you put the advice aside?

Today, consider whether or not it's too late to take action now on that guidance. Are you willing to listen to your inner voice?

TIP 6

You Are More Attractive When You Expect Breakthroughs to Look Like Breakdowns

> For every failure, there's an alternative course of action. You just have to find it. When you come to a roadblock, take a detour.
>
> *Mary Kay Ash*

IF YOU have been looking at your Strategic Attraction Plan each of the last five days, then you are seeing changes in your business starting to occur—some good, some appearing to be not so good.

Remember that your plan is always working for you, even if you do not look at it every day. With that in mind, you can expect shifts in your business to occur on a regular basis. While, at first, these shifts may not always appear as pleasant surprises, they are always working to create a bigger space into which more perfect customers can be attracted.

Today's tip is a reminder that you are more attractive when you welcome breakdowns as the first step toward experiencing breakthroughs.

Breakthroughs often look like breakdowns at the start. When you are on the brink of expanding your capacity to accomplish even greater successes, it is reasonable to expect that you may not have all the tools or the support or the information that you require when you begin.

You had no way of knowing that you were missing these details because you had no need for them before you began creating your Strategic Attraction Plan. Yet now these missing details are popping up everywhere. You may even be thinking that it will be impossible to achieve your plans because you need so much in order to move forward. It may appear as if a major obstacle is blocking your path, preventing you from proceeding further. At this point, you may feel stalled or completely stopped.

As we explored earlier, consider that what you are experiencing is much like a baby learning to walk. When you first felt the urge to move in ways that you had never done before, you watched how others stood up and walked and you believed you were ready to do the same. However, the first time you attempted such a feat, your legs were not yet sturdy enough to support you. It required a number of attempts: You got up; you fell down; you got up; you fell down; you got frustrated; you got up; you fell down; *you got up!* And after the first few tentative steps, you were more than ready to run.

Today, take a moment to envision yourself as a baby learning to walk. Consider what that baby needs in terms of support to ensure its success. Your approach to this new process of working your Strategic Attraction Plan will be completely different—perhaps more playful—after this exercise.

Or return to the vision of the lighthouse standing strong and erect on the shore as boats come and go to be served. This vision is what helped Cathy Crawford, owner of the Eagles' Nest Group, to stand out in the crowd when she experienced the breakup of her former employer, a large Internet organization. From her vantage point as one of the company's sales directors, she shares this story:

I recently chose to be a lighthouse in the midst of chaos and turmoil. My company was in the midst of a difficult merger that threw the field sales force into panic. As I stepped back to view what was happening and how my coworkers were choosing to respond, I was horrified and tempted to jump into the panic. From the perspective of synchronicity, I saw the bloody mess that is created when others act like lighthouses running up and down the beach, forgetting that they have a service to provide to the ships that rely on them. So, I gave myself permission to be the lighthouse standing firmly on the shore, shining my light so that ships may sail in my direction. Not only did this give my clients and coworkers hope, but it also gave me renewed strength and hope as well." [44]

When Jim Beckman, owner of Industrial Ecology, a waste management organization, first created his Strategic Attraction Plan, he experienced unexpected shifts firsthand:

What in the world am I doing? I don't have any clients right now. . . .

Perhaps what I'm doing is holding out for the "perfect client." I do notice that I am much less attached to acquiring just any new client. . . .

I have committed to

- have at least five phone conversations with prospects each day and discover at least one new project to quote on each day.
- mail out thank-you letters to previous customers, reminding them of our services and asking for referrals.

    ✦ print 4,000 postcards that will advertise our Web site.

    ✦ be approved as a credit card merchant and have the credit card order form fully functional by next week.[45]

Clearly, he was adjusting to the space created by the absence of clients and using the time to improve all the items he had listed as needing improvement in order to attract more perfect clients. Jim now reports,

> I have implemented an e-commerce strategy by which customers may purchase our software directly from our Internet Web site; I do call a couple of new people per week; I communicate with my favorite customers and get new and different business from them; I do refer people who do not seem to be my perfect client to other businesses in my same industry, rather than taking my time and energy to deal with them—and I am quite free to do that without feeling guilty or insulting them. The empty space in my business lasted only a month. I now have the problem of satisfying orders.[46]

Now it's your turn to consider where your business is experiencing breakdowns. Perhaps orders are not being fulfilled on time. Or you are surrounded by less-than-perfect employees and coworkers. Is your Web site server having technical difficulties? Did you recently lose a big customer—or two?

When you feel your business is flooded with breakdowns, the trick is to remember that the breakthroughs are just on the other side. The following affirmation is what helps us to keep our light shining strong and bright when everything around us seems to be shutting down. It's provided by Zoe J. Jarboe:

All is well,
Out of this happening only good can come.
Everything is still working out for my benefit.
I AM SAFE.[47]

We invite you to write this affirmation on Side #4 of your Strategic Attraction Plan as a reminder to yourself. Are you beginning to see the light shining through?

TIP 7

You Are More Attractive When You Shift the Situation

> We meet ourselves time and again in a thousand disguises on the paths of life.
>
> *Carl Jung*

MOST OF us spend much of our time figuring out how to make others act the way we want them to: How can I make my sales team close more deals? How can I make that customer sign the agreement by the end of the week? How can I get my boss off my back?

Let's experiment today with an alternative approach. Instead of working hard at changing other people, let's try shifting the situation. Shifting the situation requires us to accept the concept that other people are simply a reflection of ourselves. In other words, when we encounter someone whose behavior is either positive or offensive to us, the situation provides us an opportunity to look into our own lives to see where we are exhibiting the same behavior.

If other people are simply a reflection of us, then it stands to reason that we can change their behavior by shifting our relationship to the situation. Use this tip to assist in identifying the areas of your life and business where a shift is required so you can be even more attractive to your perfect customers and employees.

Here are the steps:

1. Think back over last week and recall a situation with a customer, employee, supervisor, or vendor that did not go the way you wanted it to go.

2. Recall how the other person behaved and how the behavior made you feel. In other words, was the person rude or late? Did she not keep her word? Was he not completely honest?

3. Write down on a piece of paper all the behaviors that this person demonstrated that you did not like. (You will not be sharing this list with the person, so be sure to write down everything—don't hold back. This is for the good of your business.)

4. Write down next to each negative behavior an opposite, positive behavior (i.e., the behavior you would have preferred). For example, if the negative behavior of this person was rudeness, then you may want to write down that you would have preferred that he or she was courteous, polite, respectful, happy, or positive. Do this for each negative behavior you have listed.

5. Transfer only the positive behaviors to Side #1 of your Strategic Attraction Plan.

You could end the exercise right here—this exercise alone will produce great advances in your business this week because you have become even clearer about the qualities that you want to have demonstrated around you. Yet your plan can take you to even greater heights if you are willing to follow the next few steps:

6. Look back over your original list of negative qualities.

7. Ask yourself if you have recently demonstrated any of these negative qualities yourself. For example, were you rude with anyone (a waitress, the driver of the car in front of you that was going too slowly, your spouse) during the last week?

8. Write down how you would prefer to behave the next time a similar situation arises.

9. Finally, forgive yourself and the person you used as your example for this exercise, and begin your relationship with yourself and with that person anew.

Dr. Robert Stecker, author of *It's U-Mail: A Lighthearted Guide for Developing and Enhancing Your Intuition*, shares his advice on how to conduct this exercise: "Another dimension to this exercise is to take the negative and positive list and put before each the phrase 'I am (X).' Often the negative qualities are those that we have had difficulty owning in the past but have now changed! The reaction of being disturbed by the other person is a nonconscious way of letting us know that a shift has occurred in us."[48]

Architect Karen Blakeman found that she shifted her world with this exercise: "Things are steadily improving for me at work. I feel that I must credit looking at my strategic plan on a daily basis with helping me to present a more positive attitude (which attracts positive) and helping me to look for more positives (thereby finding them)."[49]

Based on our own personal experience with this exercise, we can guarantee that as you shift yourself, so will those around you shift themselves. In some cases, they may detach themselves from your business easily and effortlessly. In other cases, your relationship will get better and better. Either way, your environment will improve and so will your business!

You Are More Attractive When You Acknowledge Accomplishments and Declare Completions

YOU HAVE been practicing the art of attraction for a full week. Congratulations! It's time to acknowledge your accomplishments, as well as any situations that appear to have been failures or any goals that have not yet been achieved along your path. It is very important that you continue to keep yourself fully energized so that you and your business are as attractive as possible.

> I am open and receptive to new avenues of income. I now receive my good from expected and unexpected sources. I am an unlimited being accepting from an unlimited source in an unlimited way.
>
> *Louise Hay*
> You Can Heal Your Life

In the past, you may have found that when you tended to ignore your thoughts and feelings about failures in favor of keeping "a positive mental attitude," those thoughts did not stay suppressed for very long. Instead, they appeared at the most inopportune times and caused roadblocks on your journey to success.

As you mentally and physically prepare for a new week, you may find that your "inner critic" (very different from your "inner voice") is chiding you for not yet accomplishing the goals you set for yourself.

If you listen to this inner critic, you will see yourself as a failure, which is not the best vantage point for creating your schedule for the coming week.

Today, stop for a half hour to make a list of all that you actually did accomplish in the past week. Open your daily planner and review each day. Then list all those activities, efforts, meetings, and goals that fill you with pride at their accomplishment.

Your list may look like the one compiled by Jane Boyd, author, speaker, and publisher of the Letters from Mom booklet series:

- Wrote, edited, designed, published two Letters from Mom booklets.
- Created and designed a Web site.
- Started teaching the information in my booklets at the Covenant House and the University of Texas Recovery Center.
- Interviewed by a TV syndicate, which aired on eighty TV stations across the U.S.[50]

Or it could resemble this one by Barbara Progar, a senior consultant for Mary Kay cosmetics:

- I succeeded in making it yet another year since the death of my husband.
- I succeeded in sending my legally blind high school graduate off to college.
- I succeeded in building my Mary Kay business.
- I succeeded in creating goals and dreaming dreams that I did not know lay within me.[51]

Next, list all those activities, tasks, and goals that were not accomplished this week. At the end of the list, write the following:

"Complete for the week of [date]." This is the reminder to yourself that this week is done. You accomplished what was to be done to the best of your ability, and it is now complete.

The first step toward completing your incomplete tasks is to make this list. Once it is out of your mind and onto a piece of paper, it is much easier to assign time lines for completion of these tasks. More importantly, though, once on paper, these tasks are no longer taking up precious creative space in your mind. And when you are able to use your mind for creative thinking, you are definitely more attractive, just like Robert Sgovio, owner of Integrated Life Systems, who reports, "When I began compiling my list of incompletions, I felt sad, as if I had not used my power to its full potential. Yet when I created my list of accomplishments, I had to acknowledge that some of these goals had been accomplished simply through intent and without much effort."[52]

We, too, have found that few exercises strengthen our business relationships more and fill us with as much joy as listing our accomplishments and declaring our completions at the end of each week, each month, and each year. During those times when we feel that our goals are too far in the distance, we look at our lists of accomplishments. These lists are a source of strength and encouragement. They give us the energy to keep shining our light. They keep us attractive for our most perfect clients. In fact, we often schedule a lunch meeting with our most perfect clients for the sole purpose of sharing our lists of accomplishments with them and vice versa.

If you have coworkers and employees, we recommend conducting this exercise as a team. This is an opportunity to bond at an even richer level. Create a combined list of accomplishments and post it where both your employees and your customers can easily read it—in your store, in your office, or on your Web site. This is an easy method by which to share your successes with all of your customers.

Today, we invite you to acknowledge your accomplishments and declare your unfinished business complete for the week so that tomorrow's pathway to success is free of roadblocks.

TIP 9

You Are More Attractive When You Share, Share, Share Yourself

> How do you demonstrate respect? Through the integrity of the message you communicate. It sounds simplistic, but we [at Motorola] found that the easiest way of getting things done was by being straight.
>
> *Bob Galvin*

WE BELIEVE the power of attraction lies in the sharing between two people. We encourage you today to share something with another person.

Share a referral, share a compliment, share encouragement, share your thoughts, share your feelings, share your possessions, share your time, share your love, share your knowledge, share your concerns, share your dreams, share your goals, share your questions, share your advice, share your commitment, share your spirit. The more you share yourself, the more you will come to find out about yourself.

The opportunity to share yourself with others is the object of a marvelous group game called "Who Are You?" The rules are very simple:

1. The group breaks up into pairs.
2. Each pair decides who will be Partner #1 and who will be Partner #2.

3. Partner #1 begins by asking Partner #2 the question, "Who are you?"

4. Partner #2 responds with an answer. For example, he might respond with his name.

5. Partner #1 again asks Partner #2 the question, "Who are you?"

6. Partner #2 responds with a different answer. For example, he might respond with "I am a sales manager."

7. Over a period of thirty seconds, Partner #1 continues to ask Partner #2 the question, "Who are you?" and Partner #2 continues to respond each time with a different answer.

8. At the end of the thirty-second period, Partner #1 becomes Partner #2 and vice versa. And the exercise begins again for another thirty seconds.

9. At the end of this time period, each person finds another partner, and the exercise begins again. However, this time, Partner #2 cannot use any of the answers he used in answering his first partner. He must use completely different answers.

10. Once both people in the second pairing have had a chance to be Partner #1 and Partner #2, they again choose a new partner, and the exercise begins again. Yet again, their answers to the question, "Who are you?" must not be repeated.

When employees of the same company or members of the same organization play this game, they always discover new insights about themselves and about people that they have known for a long time. Coworkers who play this game find that they let down their guard much more easily than they expect to at first and truly enjoy the process of getting to know others on a deeper and more personal level in such a short time.

Today, begin the process of calling all of your perfect customers and play this game with them. Let them know that you are interested in learning more about them in order to better serve their needs. Let them know that you want to share yourself with them so that they can know you better too.

Listen carefully to how they describe themselves. Each answer they provide is another addition to your list of perfect customer qualities. Be sure to add these qualities to your Strategic Attraction Plan before tomorrow morning.

If you are wondering what this game has to do with attracting more perfect customers, just remember that Strategic Synchronicities are produced when you first attract the most perfect customers to yourself and then continue to build strong and lasting relationships. This game is one of the most successful and fun ways for strengthening those relationships.

Just one question before we move on: Who are you?

TIP 10

You Are More Attractive When You Accept That You Don't Know

A misty morning does not signify a cloudy day.

Ancient proverb

TODAY'S TIP is about not knowing.

Have you ever noticed how often you just *know* how your day is going to go? Or you know how a person will react to a certain situation or information? Or you *know* how the traffic will be at a particular time of the day? Or you *know* what the look on a person's face means? Or you *know* that a client expects you to know all the answers ahead of time?

One example of this pattern of knowing was brought to our attention while we were teaching a class for the University of Houston's Small Business Development Center. In the middle of the class, one of the participants shared with the group that he was amazed because we were causing him to rethink everything that he thought he knew to be true about marketing. As a result, he could now see why he had not moved toward his goals as quickly as he wanted to move. We were, and continue to be, very impressed with the courage of this individual in sharing this revelation and with his willingness to suspend his "truth" in order to explore other truths on his path to success.

Today, consider the situations in your business where you just know how something is going to go, how someone is going to react, how you will respond—in other words, all the situations where you assume that you *know*. Then imagine what might be possible if you allow yourself to not know. In Zen philosophy, this is called experiencing "the beginner's mind." It's an opportunity to start fresh with an open, uncluttered mind so that there is room for new—and more fulfilling—information to be received.

When you created your Strategic Attraction Plans, you most likely accessed the "files" you have been storing for years in your mind about what you desire to have and attract. This is the information about which you *know*.

Now go to a deeper level of attraction by allowing yourself to temporarily ignore those files and let your inner voice express itself—to guide you to the next step without your having to know what that step will be before you take it. For those of you who are reading this book because you hoped it would help you "think outside of your box," this is the exercise that will help you accomplish that goal. It will provide you with velocity in making more irresistible improvements.

This exercise is the key to a successful business, according to Michael Gerber, author of the *E-Myth Revisited*, who has contributed to the reengineering of more than 15,000 businesses. He says, "the problem with most failing businesses is not that their owners don't know enough about finance, marketing, management, and operations— they don't, but those things are easy enough to learn—but that they spend their time and energy defending what they think they know. My experience has shown me that the people who are exceptionally good in business aren't so because of what they know but because of their *insatiable need to know more*."[53]

Suspending what you know and welcoming what you don't know works wonders in clearing out what doesn't work anymore and attracting what is a more perfect fit for you. To do this, you will have to call up your courage because it is uncomfortable to not know what to do next. You may feel like a four-year-old who wants to pull the covers over your head and hide. Or you may find that you want to keep yourself busy with other distractions so as to ignore your feelings of being uncomfortable and unsettled.

By avoiding the situation, though, you would be avoiding life. And to avoid life, you would have to turn off your attraction powers, which would leave you feeling powerless and completely unable to cope with the situation.

Judy Adler, a global feng shui practitioner, reports that she used to deal with facing the unknown by putting on a brave face and "acting like I know what I'm doing or joking about not knowing, or I would discover that I'm just too busy to deal with the unknown right now. Most recently I have been experimenting with the energy of the emotions that arise, such as fear or anger (which seem to be always linked). This has proven to be much more useful than the pretenses of the past. When I look at fear or anger as an energy, then I can find a way to use that energy for the good of all. The unknown becomes less intimidating and more interesting, and I find myself more vibrant, alive, attractive, productive, and easier to be around."[54]

As Judy has experienced, it's far better to trust that you have created the situation, to face it head-on and know that it is perfect because what is coming is what you want. When you practice not knowing, that is the perfect time to keep adding to your Strategic Attraction Plans.

Sam Horn, uplifting consultant, speaker, and author of *Tongue Fu!*, *ConZentration*, and *What's Holding You Back?* counsels, "If we do only what we know and 'control'—we're playing it safe, staying in our comfort zone, and doing same ole, same ole. Therefore, it's wise of us to *welcome* the unknown because it's an opportunity to be resourceful, learn, stretch, and add to our knowledge, skills, and relationships. Who *knows* whom we will meet, what we will learn, what we will experience today, tomorrow, next week?"[55] That experience is *exciting*, not frightening. The ever-unfolding newness of life is what keeps this journey fresh and perennially interesting.

Just like a good movie or book, not knowing what lies ahead adds suspense to our time here. This is the essence and potential of life, something to be embraced not feared. Knowing what happens next would make our days terribly dreary and predictable.

What helps us look forward is operating with the calm, trusting expectation that good will happen. And if good doesn't happen, we should remember the Zen saying that "All experience is education for the soul" and Auguste Rodin's quote that "Nothing is a waste of time if you use the experience wisely."

Everything that happens to us has value—if we will just look for and extract the lesson and move forward, better for having learned it. This gives us a peacefulness that prepares us for whatever occurs.

You may be pleasantly surprised by what shows up in the space of not knowing.

You Are More Attractive When You Are in the Flow

> Sometimes I go about pitying myself, and all along my soul is being blown by great winds across the sky.
>
> *Ojibway saying*

TO BE "in the flow," one must first have followed Tip 10: "You Are More Attractive When You Accept That You Don't Know." When we are able to accept that we don't have all the answers, new people and information come our way. To be in the flow, all you need to do is stop holding on to "the way that it's always been done" and trust that there is a better, easier, or more satisfying way to accomplish your goals.

In Tip 10, we recommended spending the day "not knowing," i.e., suspending having to know all the answers or be in control of all situations and then seeing what results show up in your business and your life as a result—rather a risky exercise.

Angela Caughlin, co-owner of Millennium Success Consultants, took this advice and found her way into the flow:

> Once I started realizing I was "not knowing," events started to take place that began to make me aware that my world is now operating in a different way.

My company sponsored a training class for a group of businesses. We were not thrilled with the response. During the training, I was sitting outside the room in order to greet late-comers. An Internet company was hosting a seminar in the room across from us. One of the owners of the company asked me what types of training we did. I told her, and she immediately asked me if we could put together a proposal for her company. That same day my business partner had lunch with another owner of a large company. When [the owner] realized that [my partner] had left a training seminar to have lunch with him, he immediately asked her if we could do a proposal for some training for him, as well. There were also three other companies in the seminar that asked if we could call them to discuss training needs. Synchronicity was definitely at work! And it continues!

Once I started experiencing the "flow," I began to trust that wherever I am is exactly where I am supposed to be, even if it is not exactly what I had planned. When I rely too much on my own agenda, and I'm not open to experience whatever is around me in the moment, I can break the flow. Being present in the moment allows the Universe to present me with incredible opportunities in many areas of my life.[56]

Take a moment now to turn to Side #4 of your Strategic Attraction Plan and select one of the items you listed that is in need of improvement. Are you now ready to experiment with not knowing all the answers as to how you are going to improve that item? Will you allow yourself to attract and receive answers and suggestions from others on your way to making more irresistible improvements?

If so, then get ready to flow!

You Are More Attractive When You Welcome Interruptions

Everything and everybody prospers me now.

Catherine Ponder
The Dynamic Laws of Prosperity

HAVE YOU ever experienced having to meet a deadline and feeling that anything that stopped you from meeting that deadline was wasting your time? If so, you may be pleased to know that today's tip is a short one. It will move your plan forward quickly.

As your Strategic Attraction Plan gathers energy and you become more and more successful in attracting perfect clients and customers—as well as more perfect employees, vendors, and partners—you may experience resentment toward the people and things that interfere with or interrupt you along the way. These interruptions may feel as if they are taking you out of the flow. Tip 12 will provide you with a new outlook on interruptions.

Today, treat interruptions as if they were angels with an important message, intended just for you, that is related to the very goal on which you are working to achieve.

Are you willing to join Shelly Antley, an executive recruiter in the sales and technology industries, in applying this tip to your business?

She says, "What a wonderful way to look at interruptions. I've been so frustrated recently with my inability to complete a thought without some type of interruption. And yes, I thought they were a necessary evil. Beginning today, I am going to make it a point to look for the miracle in each one."[57]

The best way that we have found to remind ourselves of this approach is to repeat the affirmation at the beginning of this tip from Catherine Ponder in her book *The Dynamic Laws of Prosperity.* Whenever we are focused on completing a project or task, we repeat again and again, "Everything and everybody prospers me now."[58]

This affirmation works best when said aloud. The more we say it, the more prosperous we feel. And we find that the only interruptions we receive are those that truly do offer a benefit or a contribution toward the completion of our project or task.

When you view interruptions in this way, you will find that you are able to stay focused no matter how often others may interfere.

You Are More Attractive When You Actively Attract Abundance

> God is my unfailing supply, and large sums of money come to me quickly, under grace, in perfect ways.
>
> *Florence Scovel Shinn*

AS WE'VE explored in detail previously, *where attention goes, energy flows.* The key questions for today are, Where is your attention? What are you expecting to see?

This is another, deeper take on Tip 12: "You Are More Attractive When You Welcome Interruptions." If we put our attention on what we consider to be "wrong" or "not quite right" in our business, such as constant interruptions, that is what we will continue to see. Is it true for you (as it is for us) that once you put your attention on something that you feel is wrong, you suddenly start to see all the other areas that are not perfect? However, when you choose to focus on the areas in business where you are pleased, do you notice that other issues tend to fall into place much more smoothly and easily?

When you start to put your attention on the areas where you are lacking, you begin a downward spiral of negativity and depression. When you start to put your attention on the areas where you have abundance, you begin an upward spiral of joy, cooperation, and prosperity.

One way to begin putting your attention on abundance is to notice the people who surround you in your office, your social circles, your community. You have access to many abundant resources through these people—for example, friendship, money, support, and technical knowledge. By recalling that the first principle of attraction is to notice the positive qualities in the people around you, you can see how essential it is to also focus on the abundant resources that surround you.

Today, make a list of the resources that are in abundance in the people that surround you. To help you get started, we are sharing with you the lists of abundant resources that have been compiled by some of your fellow Synchronicity Strategists.

Heather Leah Smith, ERP (enterprise resource planning) senior manager for First Consulting Group, writes, "I experience an abundance of brilliance around me. I have the awesome privilege of working with people who are brilliant and have the ability to create a solution to any challenge that has faced us on this project within twenty-four hours. They have been amazing to watch. I have an abundance of friends and family members that truly honor the path that I am on and want me to be happy."[59]

Lynn W. Ellis, CCAS, C.P.M., regional director for the Indiana Government Marketing Assistance Group, relates, "The most abundant resource at my workplace is the knowledge that each person possesses and the contribution that each makes to the whole in making a project, an assignment, a task successful. It is amazing what each person can contribute to a project so that it is accomplished in a timely fashion, in an above average manner, and to meet the needs and demands of those persons we are servicing."[60]

Ed Young, president of Edwin G. Young II Insurance Agency, writes, "The exploring for resources all around us is interesting. Certainly friendships are crucial to confirm and affirm our value to others and to acknowledge our humanness. This was brought home to me yesterday when I was having lunch with a friend who allowed me to share feelings and concerns that I wouldn't share with just anyone. I was able to go back to my office feeling refreshed and perhaps more attractive."[61]

Wayne Springer, president of Atiwa Computing, includes on his list "An absolute abundance of helpful people around me. An absolute abundance of things that make me laugh every day and provide me with great stories."[62]

Now it's your turn. What are the resources that surround you throughout your day? Begin to write a list of these abundant resources. How many items can you list—three, seven, more than ten?

Keep this list handy, and the next time you are interrupted you might find it easier to remember that the person standing before you or calling on the phone or sending you an e-mail—rather than being a hindrance—is actually one more abundant resource.

TIP 14

You Are More Attractive When You Delight in the Success of Others

THE TIP today encourages us to be "legacy builders." Legacy building means spreading positive words and good thoughts about someone else.

We encourage you to make a commitment to surround yourself with people who are successful and to bask in their success. If you agree that others are simply a reflection of ourselves, then you would also agree that the success of others is actually your success, too. In addition, their success provides you with an opportunity to envision even greater successes that you want to achieve.

Your commitment will attract many opportunities for practicing this tip. Your first tendency may be to compare yourself with the other person—actually, to envy him or her—a very human way to behave. That tendency, however, will prevent you from being completely happy for the person's success, and it will block you from accessing the positive energy that is available when success is present.

> True modesty and true pride are much the same thing: both consist in setting a just value on ourselves— neither more nor less.
>
> *William Hazlitt*

James Doyle of Bartlett Tree Experts is a master of legacy build-ing. He believes that referrals are very important and effective because most of us have a difficult time bragging about ourselves. We have been taught that it's not polite or nice to boast about our successes. As a result, we may feel uncomfortable to hear people speaking about their successes. This discomfort is the reason why the most success-ful advertising and promotion campaigns are focused on the *benefits* consultants or companies provide to customers, as opposed to brag-ging about how much better they are than the competition.

Based on that concept, it seems reasonable that the most suc-cessful way for our businesses to grow is through the good words that our perfect customers and others say about us. Upon further reflec-tion, the Golden Rule springs to mind: "Do unto others as you would have them do unto you." In other words, if you desire to have others spread news of your business, then you have a responsibility to spread good news of their businesses, too.

By now, most of us have had the experience of sharing with our perfect customers the qualities and attributes that we most admire about them. The next step is to go out into the world with the intention of legacy building for their businesses.

Today, become a legacy-builder—bask in the glory of your cus-tomers', coworkers', and associates' successes, and brag about their successes to others.

One particularly rewarding way to be a legacy builder is to arrange a celebration lunch for one of your perfect customers and a member of the business community that your customer would like to get to know. The purpose of the lunch would be for you to brag about this perfect customer and his or her company as a means of spreading the legacy further into the community.

As Pamela Grant, owner of Career Callings, reports, "Celebration is a vital part of life. If we celebrate all our successes, we will tend to remember them twice as much as our fears! Therefore, we will attract even more success. Remember—what we think about, expands! I celebrate all of my associates during this and every day!"[63]

Can you imagine how much stronger and satisfying your relationships with your perfect customers and others can be when you commit to be a legacy builder for them and their businesses?

For whom are you legacy building today?

You Are More Attractive When You Take Immediate Action

> Make no little plans; they have
> no magic to stir men's blood. . . .
> Make big plans, aim high
> in hope, and work.
>
> *Daniel H. Burnham*

YOU HAVE now been practicing the process of attraction for a full two weeks—or have you? Perhaps you have been coasting along, simply reading the tip for each day instead of actually putting into action the daily exercises, which provide the fuel for your Strategic Attraction Plans.

Either way, as you enter into your third week of attracting more perfect clients and customers, it is now time to take immediate action. Why? Because there is power in taking immediate action. And self-empowerment is very attractive.

The process of strategic attraction is based on planning. However, the planning is for naught unless we put ourselves into action.

Some powerful actions that we have previously explored and that you may wish to take now are these:

1. Look at your plan every morning for five minutes. Keep it in a place where you must see it every morning—on your bathroom mirror, in your day planner, or on your computer.

2. Keep adding qualities and attributes to your perfect customer or other "perfect" list. You can challenge yourself to see how many new qualities and attributes you can add each day, each week, or each month. Then, go through your database of all of your customers and review how closely each one matches the list of perfect qualities.

3. Call all of your perfect customers and take each one to coffee or lunch on a regular basis to keep building your relationship outside the normal routine of business. To do this every quarter is a good rule of thumb. Keep sharing with your perfect customers the additions you have made to your plan, and continue to ask them to support you in attracting more people with whom you would enjoy working. Of course, these meetings are a great opportunity to find out how you can continue to be of service to them, too.

4. Each day, select one item from your list of what you must improve and make one improvement in that area.

5. Complete at least one incomplete task each day. When you are able to accomplish an outstanding task, you receive a euphoric sense of success, which makes you even more attractive to others.

By now your plan is beginning to stir up your business. As a result, you may feel that you are too busy to take any of these actions on a consistent basis—including looking at your plan every day!

This is the point where you get to choose how you want your business to be. By keeping your commitment to yourself to look at your plan every morning, you allow yourself to stay clear about where your business is heading. When you do this consistently, you will notice that the other actions on the list above occur naturally, easily, and effortlessly. The amount of time spent taking actions that are not in line with your Strategic Attraction Plan will gradually diminish. You will stop attracting less-than-perfect clients, you will enjoy the work that you do each day, and you will have fun again!

Before you turn another page, *stop*. Look at your Strategic Attraction Plan for five minutes. If you have multiple plans, look at each one for five minutes. What one additional action do you need to take to move each plan forward immediately?

TIP 16

You Are More Attractive When You Establish Your Expertise

> A wise man will make more opportunities than he finds.
>
> *Francis Bacon*

WITH YOUR powers of attraction in full force today, it is time to envision yourself as an expert about your industry.

In the Strategic Attraction Planning Process, nothing is as attractive as providing education. The more opportunities you have to educate someone else about your industry, the more attractive you become. One of the best venues for sharing your knowledge is through involvement with networking groups and organizations. If you already belong to at least one referral club, networking group, or business-related organization, great!

Today, offer yourself as a speaker to other networking groups. You have expertise about your field that members of these groups would love to have from you.

When you establish yourself as a speaker with industry expertise, you actually become a beacon of light in the dark haze of confusion that many of your potentially perfect customers experience day to day. Like boats to a lighthouse, the right people will be attracted to you, especially since you are making it easy for them to receive your knowledge and to ask questions of you. Most importantly, you are planting yourself on the shore where they are looking to find you.

You may think it's a bit daunting to speak to a large group of people. But before you dismiss this tip because you feel you are unqualified to speak as an expert, keep reading.

The best way to make the experience of speaking more comfortable is to speak on a topic with which you are most familiar, one that you enjoy speaking about. Take a moment now to consider what topic about your industry you enjoy most. Next, think about what topics your potentially perfect clients would want to know more about. Write those topics down.

When you finish reading today's tip, call your current perfect customers to see if they agree with the topics you listed. Ask them to provide recommendations for other topics they want to hear you speak about. Be sure to ask them which networking groups they belong to and if those groups are looking for speakers. Then ask them who you would contact to schedule yourself as a speaker. We know this process works because this is exactly how we began our speaking careers.

To improve your speaking skills, we recommend that you join Toastmasters International (www.toastmasters.org). The mission of Toastmasters International is as follows: "Whether you're a professional, student, stay-at-home parent, or retiree, Toastmasters is the best way to improve your communication skills. Toastmasters can help you lose the fear of public speaking and learn skills that will help you be more successful in whatever path you've chosen. You'll be a better listener. You'll easily lead teams and conduct meetings. You'll comfortably give and receive constructive evaluation. You already have some or all of these skills. In Toastmasters, you will enhance them."[64]

Stacey declares that her participation in Toastmasters cured her fear of public speaking. Toastmasters groups exist all over the world, and we encourage you to visit a chapter in your town.

If you are already comfortable speaking to groups, then you are ready to participate in your local chapter of the National Speakers Association (www.nsaspeaker.org). The NSA is known as "the premier association for experts who speak professionally."[65] This is one of the most supportive and nurturing groups of people we have ever had the pleasure to know.

Both of these organizations are perfect places to meet other businesspeople just like yourself with whom you can share leads, referrals, and information. We invite you to visit both organizations' Web sites today to find out how they can help you to establish yourself as an expert.

TIP 17

You Are More Attractive When You Clear a Space in Which to Create

STRATEGIC SYNCHRONICITIES are produced in clear, uncluttered spaces. In order for our perfect customers to easily find us, we have to stand out in a crowd. The best way to accomplish this is to be surrounded by clear space—both physically and metaphorically.

There is an ancient metaphysical law that says if we desire more abundance in our lives we must create a vacuum to allow ourselves to receive the good we seek. How can more good come into our lives if there is no room for it?

Sarah Ban Breathnach

Today, we will take a more active approach to bringing in more perfect customers by clearing a space in which to receive them.

What works best for Jan is for her to schedule time on her calendar every day for clearing off her desk, purging her files, and cleaning out her car. It's a way of clearing a space in her schedule to catch her breath. When she is breathing freely, then she is thinking more clearly, which automatically makes her more attractive.

Stacey has adopted the monthly practice of finding twenty-seven items in her office that she can give away or throw away as a means of creating a void to be filled with something better. For this tip, she acknowledges Suze Orman and her book *The Courage to Be Rich.*[66]

From a pragmatic standpoint, these practices allow us to have an office space that we are proud to share with and show to others—one that is a true representation of the clarity that we provide to our clients.

Today, ask yourself what might be possible if you were to clear a space for anything you want to come into your life and your business. We asked this question of a number of Synchronicity Strategists. See if any of their replies resembles your response.

George Phares, president of Strategic Direction Resources, writes:

> My mailbox is full of old notes, our files have twelve months of data, and my desk has stacks of magazines that resemble canyon walls. Now is the time to review what is important (to us and our clients), be grateful for what has come our way over the past year, and let go of that which we no longer need. As I read those old notes I've saved, I remember why they came my way, am grateful for the value in them, and then free myself from the clutter.[67]

Evalyn Shea, owner of Shea Writing Solutions, states:

> I find myself in a sea of paper in both my home and work offices! The paper has overflowed to the floor in my home office (this is indeed sad as I have a fair amount of space available there) and it covers my desk and credenza in the office. I have lost track of important papers because they are all "out" on the surface where I continuously reshuffle and repile them.
>
> As I walked in to the office this morning, I resolved that the first thing I will do is clean up the mess.[68]

Pamela Terry, an account executive in the telecommunications industry, writes:

> Here are some tips that I use to keep my car in shape:
>
> I purchase a month's worth of car washes at a time. That motivates me to get my car washed often so that I get my money's worth. . . . I end up washing my car about once a week to two weeks—which also forces me to straighten all the stuff. This has been the best technique so far that I have found. I have a sport utility vehicle, so I use the very back of it to store items that I am transporting. I have a plastic box for my cassette tapes, and I have a straw bag that closes in which I put those things I am transporting.[69]

Take a moment now to identify where your life and your business are cluttered. Once you have identified an item to dispose of, throw it away, give it away, or find a use for it by the end of the day. Give yourself space in which to sort out what you want to take with you into the future and what you want to leave behind.

You Are More Attractive
When You Have a Field Day

> You can't climb uphill by
> thinking downhill thoughts.
>
> *Anonymous*

After more than two weeks using the Strategic Attraction Planning Process, you are beginning to experience success in producing results. You may have attracted a number of new perfect customers, the relationships with your existing customers may be improving, or you may have noticed that your attitude and approach to your work is more positive.

These are indicators that you are becoming successful in mastering the attraction process. How does it feel? Are you comfortable with the changes, or do they feel uncomfortable? Is everything flowing smoothly, or are you feeling overwhelmed and out of control? Are you beginning to worry about how you will meet the demand if business continues to go so well?

Synchronicity Strategists often find at this point that their plans are producing much greater success than they had ever experienced before. When we get close to success, staring it in the face can be frightening. When we see that we can realize our wildest dreams, often we don't know what to do with the success. It's a new feeling, and it's uncomfortable and unsettling.

Success scares us because we can't control it. Our life and our business are taking off on their own. We don't need to worry about them or work hard on their behalf—and they definitely don't need us to struggle. So there's nothing for us to do. As bizarre as it may seem, we may even experience a feeling of being left out of our own life!

Confronted with such a frightening feeling, our tendency is to struggle to find a way to get back to a place of concern. That often means finding something to complain about or worry about. Maybe we worry about what will happen if our plans don't succeed. Or we worry about being able to handle all the business coming our way. Whatever we choose to worry about, the worry is simply an indicator that we'd rather stick with what's familiar than enjoy and capitalize on the possibilities that grow out of our success. The fact that fear and worry are the most common responses to success may be the fundamental reason why most people never actually achieve their dreams.

Remember, you are more attractive when you are enjoying and delighting in your successes. Yes, you may have a few new details to work out. You may have to hire more people or create a new system or learn additional skills. The easiest way of managing these elements, though, is simply to write them on Side #4 of your Strategic Attraction Plan—"What Do I Have to Improve?"

The exercise today is to allow yourself to take a twenty-four-hour break from fear of the future—to have a field day with your success. What might be possible if, during those twenty-four hours, you allow yourself to play with the notion of how wonderful it is that you are experiencing success today? What if, for twenty-four hours, you simply trust that your Strategic Attraction Plan will ensure that you can handle whatever the future may bring? Can you stand a full twenty-four hours of success?

Will you join us in having a field day?

You Are More Attractive When You Break Bread with a Competitor

> We have met the enemy,
>
> and it is us.
>
> *Pogo (Walt Kelly)*

THE TIP today is a bit outrageous: call one of your competitors and invite him or her to lunch with the goal of transforming this competitor into a collaborator.

As a Synchronicity Strategist, you should always be prepared to refer less-than-perfect clients to someone else in your industry for whom they are more perfect. The only way to truly know your competitors is to build relationships with them.

We have worked with many clients who, at first, balked at this tip. They believed that the owners of the other businesses in their industry would not want to share any information with a so-called competitor. Our advice to them and to you is to begin developing relationships with businesspeople who belong to your industry's trade association. These are the people who understand the importance of sharing knowledge, information, and even customers for the betterment of all concerned. Most of the local chapters of these associations have monthly breakfast or lunch meetings specifically for the purpose of introducing representatives of competitive businesses to each other.

If you already belong to a trade association, then we encourage you to get to know better those members with whom you do not often associate.

With this exercise, it is important to go beyond your comfort zone. This may sound like a contradiction to the Synchronicity Standard of staying true to your mission, but you have to explore the missions of other businesses in order to know how they are different from yours. Although this exploration can be uncomfortable, it can also be exciting, invigorating, and eye-opening.

For this exercise to produce the intended results, you must seek out representatives of competitive businesses whom you would normally not have an interest in knowing better. The idea is to learn more about businesses in the same industry with missions that are different from yours. Remember that there is nothing wrong with the way that other businesses operate; they are just different from the way you operate.

It is just as important to undertake this exploration within your own company, especially if you are a member of a sales team. Sometimes it may make more sense for another person on your team to serve a customer in your territory. Why? Because that salesperson may have a better rapport with the customer than you do. In the long run, it's more rewarding for you to ensure that customers are being served by their most perfect vendor.

Take a moment now to consider how many close relationships you have with other businesspeople or your own coworkers to whom you can refer prospects that are not perfect for you to serve. Imagine how enjoyable it could be to make referrals to other businesses without hesitation at the very moment your inner voice lets you know that a prospect is not meant for you.

Imagine being a hero to the prospects because you have shown them that you have their best interests in mind. And imagine keeping your own space clear so that you can attract the most profitable and enjoyable customers for you to serve!

Which competitor will you take to lunch today?

TIP 20

You Are More Attractive When You Gain Clarity About Yourself

> One's own self is well hidden from one's own self. Of all mines of treasure, one's own is the last to be unearthed.
>
> *Friedrich Nietzsche*

AS YOU have been creating your Strategic Attraction Plans, you have been honing your abilities and capacities for manifesting what you want in the world. This is quite a powerful attribute. Yet it's been developing within you on a very subtle level, so quietly that you might not realize how different you are becoming to those around you.

Your first clue of this change may be that you find yourself becoming frustrated that your customers, your business partners, your employees, and your vendors "just don't get it." Are you feeling like this now?

We strongly believe that whenever we find ourselves being frustrated by something that someone else does or says, the situation is occurring for a specific reason. We attracted it into our world for our growth.

Remember, you have the ability to manifest anything you want by first becoming clear about how you want it to look when it does manifest itself. So if you are frustrated by a situation—perhaps your customer wants a discount that you feel is unjustified—all you have to do is recognize that you can shift the situation by getting clear about the outcome that you want to achieve. If you want the customer to understand that you are not willing to provide the discount, then you must first become clear about that fact yourself so that you can explain it clearly to your customer. Then the customer is free to make his or her own choice as to whether or not you are his or her perfect vendor.

Your clarity will give others the freedom to express what they want, too. And from this open, clear, and honest communication, a new possibility for the relationship will emerge—a true shift in the situation.

For example, one of our clients, a consultant herself, shared with us that she was concerned about the way she ended an assignment for one of her clients. This business owner had changed from being a perfect customer at the start of the assignment to one who was definitely less than perfect by the end. Yet the consultant did not know why. Upon learning this tip, she decided to invite her client to lunch to find out what worked and what did not work about the way she handled the assignment. She also intended to share her thoughts about what worked and what did not work for her in relation to working with him.

At the end of the lunch, after clearing the air and clarifying a series of misunderstandings, the consultant realized she simply had not clearly stated to her client at the beginning of the project the services he could expect her to provide and what she expected of him as a client. Her client was so pleased with the quality and clarity of the conversation that he gave her another, more perfect assignment to manage for his company.

Your ability to be clear about what you want your perfect customers to expect of you is what makes the difference.

Take a few minutes to review Side #3 of your Strategic Attraction Plan today. Have you clearly stated for yourself what you want your most perfect customers to expect of you? What items will you now add to this list? This list should be at least as long as the list of your perfect customer's qualities on Side #1 so that you are the perfect match for that perfect customer.

TIP 21

You Are More Attractive When You Watch for Previews of Coming Attractions

AS YOU complete your third week practicing these tips, watch for "previews of coming attractions." This is another way of stating the concept of "signs of land," which, according to Florence Scovel Shinn,[70] are confirmations from the universe that our Strategic Attraction Plans are working.

As you set out on your journey toward your goals, the destination appears to be a long way off in the distance. As you progress on your journey, you

> Leaders know some things and foresee some things which those they are presuming to lead do not know or foresee as clearly. This is partly what gives leaders their "lead," what puts them out ahead and qualifies them to show the way.
>
> *Robert K. Greenleaf*
> Servant Leadership: A Journey into the Nature of Legitimate Power and Greatness

will reach a point where you can no longer see the land that you have left behind and you cannot yet see the land to which you are heading. Just when you begin to feel lost and adrift, you will receive "signs of land," or "previews of coming attractions," to let you know you are still on the right path and getting close to your goal.[71]

Today, take a moment to consider a situation in the past that appeared to be a setback or a failure in your business when it actually might have been simply a preview of coming attractions. Perhaps you set a goal of receiving $25,000 in personal income and you received only $18,000. Or you planned to attract 1,000 more customers to your Web site and you attracted only 350. Can you now choose to see the situation as a preview of the full-length feature that is still to come, that perhaps you just miscalculated how long it would take you to reach your destination?

One of our clients, a doctor, undertook a goal to upgrade the quality and expertise of his staff. He created a Strategic Attraction Plan for attracting the most perfect employees who fit his vision and the mission of his practice. In so doing, he knew that some of his current employees would have to leave their positions to make way for his perfect staff members. Through pure intention, and by looking at his plan every day, he was able to fill these positions easily as one by one his less-than-perfect employees submitted their resignations, having found more perfect positions elsewhere.

At the end of ten months, just one position was left to be filled. This position happened to be a very key one, which once filled would allow the doctor more freedom to pursue the next stage of his plan. After numerous interviews with potential applicants, he found a person who was "almost perfect" and he hired her. However, she did not meet his "perfect employee profile" in two areas.

She stayed with his company for two weeks. During that time, she displayed all the qualities that he desired for that position, she bonded quickly with her fellow employees, and his clients liked her immediately. It appeared that she was a perfect match for all—until this employee submitted her resignation because of issues that were directly related to the areas where she did not meet the doctor's profile. Her resignation came suddenly, and it could have been a setback for any other practice. However, the doctor realized that this employee was simply a preview of coming attractions, an opportunity to experience what the business would be like once that position was filled with the perfect person. In other words, he received a confirmation that he was on the right course and that his final destination was near.

This confirmation and his belief in his Strategic Attraction Plan produced an even more perfect applicant the very next day. He hired her immediately, and the practice never skipped a beat.

You are the director of your own full-length feature about the future of your business. Keep those cameras rolling by looking at your plan every day for five minutes and trust that what you attract are the previews of what is yet to come.

BONUS TIP 1

"Ask-Offer-Thank"

Donna Fisher

IMAGINE WHAT would happen if in every conversation you asked for something, offered something, and thanked the other person for his or her support and contribution to your life!

Today, we will be experimenting with the process of "Ask-Offer-Thank." This process keeps the flow of networking present in every conversation, it creates stronger relationships, and it provides a ripple effect of opportunities.

> We can't look out for "number one" because there is no number one! The world is a team.
>
> *Ron McCann and Joe Vitale*
> The Joy of Service

It will take some courage and creativity on your part to always be prepared to ask for something. Yet the asking is what creates trust and opens the door to results. The power is in having all three components present in every conversation so that you are served, the other person is honored, and gratitude is expressed.

Donna Fisher, Certified Speaking Professional, is the author of *People Power, Power Networking, Power NetWeaving,* and *Professional Networking for Dummies* (www.donnafisher.com, Connecting Business with People and People with Life!).

168

To put this process into practice, make a list of resources you need and the contributions you can offer. Then, in every conversation, pay attention to what the other person is saying and which request and offer are a fit for that conversation.

When you're not sure what to offer, you can say, "I'd like to be of help in some way. What can I do for you?"

When you're not sure what to ask for, you can say, "I'm focused on accomplishing this task this week. Do you have any suggestions for me?"

The thanks part should be easy to accomplish. Thank people for their time, their friendship, their business, their support. Take a moment to identify what you appreciate about them and the conversation that you had with them, and be sure to thank them for the gift of their support.

As a reminder to yourself, write the phrase "Ask-Offer-Thank" on Side #3 of your Strategic Attraction Plan and look at it throughout the day. Then, just be aware and ready for your relationships, joy, and opportunities to accelerate!

Project Your Light Further

Doug Upchurch

> We have all kinds of navigational equipment—satellites, Lorans, depth sounders, compasses— all these wonderful things. But when your eye sees that lighthouse at night, you know where you are.
>
> *Rick Amory*

ONCE YOUR organization has created its Strategic Attraction Plans to become like a lighthouse standing bright and steady on the shore, guiding the perfect customers safely and securely to its harbor, it then becomes exciting to explore ways of projecting its beam of light even further.

This exploration begins with the consideration of what role technology will play in your company's strategic attraction process. For example, rather than putting time, energy, and money into doing business on-line, your company may prefer to distinguish itself by putting its emphasis on personal human contact. If, however, your perfect customers are leaders in the technology industry, they would expect their vendors to be similarly as adept and sophisticated in their use of technology.

Doug Upchurch is CEO of Insights Austin.

This is why it is very important for your company to have clarity as to the level of technology sophistication that you want your most perfect customers to possess before you begin investing your organization's time, energy, and money into its own technology infrastructure.

The "Attractive" Internet

Over the past twenty-five years, the growth of technology has exploded us into the new world of cyberspace, where we use electronic bits and bytes to represent our thoughts, words, and even our most heartfelt emotions and desires. This technology can make the light from our lighthouse so bright that perfect customers from all over the world can be attracted to us instantaneously.

The World Wide Web is an electronic ocean on which people surf and sail with the intent to reach new harbors where they can collaborate, learn, and share with others. It's a marketplace where we purchase goods and services. It's a library where we look up needed information. It's a phone book where customers find vendors. It's even a social center where people make new friends.

By knowing where to shine your light across this vast ocean, you make it easy for more perfect customers to make their way to your shore.

The way to help these perfect customers find and communicate with you via the World Wide Web is to ensure that every word, picture, and feature is in alignment with your Strategic Attraction Plan. Here are some issues to think about with regard to your Web site:

1. Does your Web site include pictures that represent your perfect customers in the perfect transaction with you? Remember, a picture is worth a thousand words. Help your customers identify with the people featured on your site.

2. Does your Web site include text that helps site visitors understand who your perfect customers are and what services and products you will provide for them? Provide case studies and customer testimonials explaining how your company created a perfect solution for them.

3. Is the text written in the language of your perfect customers? Is it too technical for your perfect customer—or not technical enough?

4. Does your Web site use technology that is easy for your perfect customers to use? If your Web site includes extra features, "bells and whistles," make sure your perfect customers are people or companies that expect your Web site to have these features and have the technology to easily view these special features.

5. Does your Web site speak to what makes your most perfect customers "tick"?

For your Web site to be a cyber-lighthouse, its content, design, and technology must all be in alignment with your Strategic Attraction Plan. One way to know if it is in alignment is to ask your perfect customers to do an analysis of your Web site in relation to all three of these areas—content, design, and technology—and to give you feedback as to what they would prefer to see. The information you receive could lead to great insights.

The next question to consider is, How will my perfect customers find my Web site? With the advent of search engines and link exchanges, the options are many.

One of the primary ways that people find Web sites on the Internet is through the use of search engines. Here's a list of just a few of the more popular search engines: Yahoo! (www.yahoo.com),

MSN (www.msn.com), Excite (www.excite.com), Northern Light (www.northernlight.com), Google (www.google.com), GoTo (www.goto.com), AltaVista (www.altavista.com), and Lycos (www.lycos.com).

The value of a search engine is that it quickly locates all Web sites related to a certain topic. As most of these search engines provide a basic listing for free, it would seem to make sense to list your company's Web site with each one of them. Before posting your company, though, your most important consideration is to identify the key words that your most perfect customers will use to reach your Web site through these search engines. Your company's basic listing will include very few words, so you will want to make sure that every word counts in order to bring the greatest number of potentially perfect customers to your site. Too often, companies include their product names and internal jargon or "buzz words" in their listings and then wonder why they are not receiving many visitors to their sites.

Long before customers know that your Web site exists, they know they have a problem they want solved. They are looking for the perfect solution to that problem. To make it easy for them to find you, make sure your listing refers to their problem. For example, let's say your company has a product called "The Revenue Booster" that helps other companies increase their profits. Potentially perfect customers are companies that want to increase profitability. An "attractive" listing on the search engines could be "Boost Revenue and Increase Profit."

Another way that customers might find you is through link exchanges with other sites that your potentially perfect customers visit. The best way to find these sites is to use a search engine yourself to locate those sites that are promoting the same benefits as your company.

As was discussed in chapter 4, collaboration allows us to serve more of our most perfect customers more perfectly. By placing a link on another company's site and reciprocating by placing its link on your Web site, you both benefit. You are both helping customers, who have very limited time to extensively explore the World Wide Web, to find both of you easily and quickly. If they find one of you, then they have found the other, too.

From Mass Messages to "Attractive" Messages

Internet technology has also given us a concept called "mass customization." Mass customization provides organizations with the ability to tailor their products or services to each and every customer, no matter how large the customer base. Amazon.com has taken full advantage of mass customization. Every time I visit this site I am greeted with a list of book recommendations that were picked just for me based on my previous purchases and searches on this site.

When you develop your first Strategic Attraction Plan, you may find that you have more than one group of perfect customers that are fairly distinct from each other. Technology has made it possible to create customized Web sites for each of these distinct perfect customer groups, almost like different storefronts for specific types of customers. By creating customized Web sites, you are able to meet the needs of each of these different groups at the same time. Perhaps some of your perfect customer groups are technical professionals who purchase your technical training services, and another group consists of human relations and training managers who purchase your team and communications training products. Custom Web sites can assist you in more specifically serving the needs of these two different groups without watering down the message for either one.

"Your Perfect Customer Is Holding on Line One"

With so much attention focused on the Internet, it's easy to lose sight of the importance of the other communication tools that make it possible for us to serve our most perfect customers. The question is simply this: How do you want your most perfect customers to contact you and when?

We'll start with telephones, mobile phones, pagers, and fax machines. Let's explore how your telecommunications plan is in alignment with your Strategic Attraction Plan.

What does your "on-hold" or outgoing greeting tell callers about your organization? Does your telephone answering system provide callers with a message that shares your organization's mission of service? What about your fax cover sheet? Does it include such a message?

I remember the first time that I called PerfectCustomers Unlimited after briefly meeting Jan and Stacey at a trade show. Although I received a voice mail message, I was excited to hear that they were "looking forward to assisting me in attracting my perfect customers." When I heard that message, I knew I had called the right company to assist me in becoming more effective in building my business.

This is a reminder that it is always important to let everyone know how you serve your perfect customers, whether they hear the message while on hold or read it on your fax cover page or at the bottom of your e-mail messages.

Next, consider how certain telephone features, such as call waiting, call forwarding, and three-way calling, fit into the needs and expectations that you want your perfect customers to have. If you want them to expect that it is easy to contact you directly, then your organization may want to invest in a toll-free phone number. If you and your staff are out of the office frequently, you may prefer for your customers to reach you via pager or cell phone or to simply leave a message at the office number so that you can call them back at your convenience. If you and your staff have cell phones, give thought to whether or not you want every customer to have the phone numbers or if it would be more perfect to share the numbers selectively.

Although these may seem like very simple and everyday issues, these issues grow in importance when put into the context that they represent the primary means of attraction that your organization uses to send its light out to its most perfect and potentially perfect customers.

"You've Got Attractive Mail"

Many of the same concepts apply when using e-mail to communicate as well. This technology provides us with new opportunities to increase our attractiveness. Take a moment to consider the following:

1. Does your e-mail signature reflect what you are seeking to attract?

2. How often do you intend to check and respond to e-mail?

3. Do you want prospects and customers to contact you by e-mail first or by phone?

4. Are the fonts and colors you use in your e-mails easy for your most perfect customers to read?

5. Do you want to send and receive e-mail file attachments?

For example, I am perfectly comfortable having my perfect customers communicate with me via e-mail or by phone. In comparison, an associate who owns a Web design company prefers to receive only e-mail communications. This allows him an opportunity to review the request and reply in a timely and effective manner at his convenience.

If you are going to make e-mail a significant part of your communication plan, then be sure your company responds in a timely manner to the e-mails it receives. Then, periodically, check with your perfect customers to make sure that your e-mails are getting through and being received as expected. Inquire as to how quickly they are receiving the e-mails your company sends. On my current system, I can send an e-mail and have it be received within seconds. On a previous system, it could take thirty minutes or more. If you want your perfect customers to expect e-mail responses to their questions within fifteen minutes yet it takes your system one hour to send your replies, then you must improve your server's capabilities. In the meantime, you might want to pick up the phone instead.

In conclusion, I am inviting you to review your technology and communications processes to determine if they are serving your most perfect customers by extending your organization's light to safely guide them to your door, your phone, or your Web site.

Synchronicity Leaders

As resources along your path to becoming a master of Strategic Synchronicity, we are introducing to you the following Synchronicity Strategists, who have completed our Synchronicity Leadership Program.

Synchronicity Leaders are consultants, trainers, or corporate executives who are committed to immersing themselves in the Strategic Attraction Planning Process. They have obtained mastery in the process, and they are grounded in the skills and have our endorsement to provide this training to their clients, coworkers, and employees.

If you find that you feel a "spark of synchronicity" reading their mission statements, feel free to contact them directly to make a connection. They welcome your questions and comments.

Eva Archer-Smith, Executive and Spiritual Life Coach
Houston, Texas • 713-528-7020 • evaas@earthlink.net

My *mission* is to support you in fully living your purpose and your passion, as an objective, yet completely committed, thinking and listening partner, I help you move to new levels of clarity, connection, joy, and power in your life.

My *perfect customer* is a person committed to personal growth and open to new and innovative ways of looking at what is possible. They want to live life to the fullest and are willing to move beyond their comfort zone to get unstuck and achieve profound breakthroughs. They have a sense of humor and adventure, and understand the importance of cultivating a rich inner life. They recognize the power that is available to them through clarity, conversation, and connection. And, they are willing to listen . . . to themselves, to me, and to the voice of synchronicity.

Laura Arellano
Meta~Logia Consulting
Leadership Development and Training
Salt Lake City, Utah ◆ 801-815-1992
arellano@relia.net ◆ www.metalogiaconsulting.com

My *mission* is fulfilling my desire for contribution by providing others with Whole Life Skills: an opportunity of awareness and development that enhances my clients' quality of life with professional skill development that crosses over to their personal lives.

From Latin, *meta* translates as "shifts" or "higher levels" and *logia* as "learning." Meta~Logia assists corporate groups and teams in increasing their success through Leadership Development and Training. I work in partnership with organizations to create and customize solutions to their employee development needs.

My *perfect customers* are businesses that demonstrate their commitment to their employees through understanding and supporting the benefits of investing in the growth and development of their people. They agree with the philosophy that learning and retention should be fun and have an abundance mindset. Their core gauge for success and personal motivation matches mine: being and bringing joy and love and making a difference through contribution.

Janet Bray Attwood, President
The Millionaire Eagles Program – Creating Enlightened
    Millionaires
108 W. Palm Drive, Suite 205 ◆ Fairfield, Iowa 52556
1-800-975-9295 ◆ janet.attwood@milleagles.com
www.milleagles.com

My *mission* is to change the economic history of the planet by creating 100 Enlightened Millionaires in 100 cities in the U.S. and Canada. An Enlightened Millionaire is someone who understands that there is no limit to the abundance in the universe, and that there is enough for everyone. An Enlightened Millionaire lives in balance, and is devoted to sharing abundance through service. They are constantly applying creativity to everyday needs, which is the basis of providing value, which in turn creates wealth, and allows the Enlightened Millionaire to give their unique gift to their families, their communities and the world.

My *perfect customer* is anyone who has the desire to become an Enlightened Millionaire and is willing to follow the simple instructions available in Mark Victor Hansen (Best selling author of the "Chicken Soup" Series) and Robert G. Allen's (four-time *New York Times* bestselling author) Millionaire Eagle Program.

Jane Boyd, Author, Speaker, Trainer
"Letters from Mom" Booklets/Workbooks and Curriculum
Houston, Texas ✦ 713-334-3370
jane@lettersfrommom.com ✦ www.lettersfrommom.com

My *mission* is to help teens and young adults discover they have the power to create the life of their dreams.

My *perfect customers* are parent groups of teens and any organizations working with, counseling, or mentoring teens. These organizations are looking for multiple topic curriculum, resources and train-the-trainer sessions to help teens become confident, productive and self-sufficient. The parent groups of teens are looking for help, training and resources to help them live with and raise their teens. All groups and organizations are easy to work with, have realistic expectations and want a win-win relationship. They will be so pleased with the curriculum that they easily and gladly refer me to other organizations for speaking, teaching, and training opportunities.

Maria Carter
Fall In Love With Your Life
San Diego, California ✦ maria@fallinlovewithyourlife.com
www.mariacarter.com

My *mission* is to Love and to help others Love more fully.

My *perfect customers* are individuals who want to experience more love, laughter, and prosperity in their personal and business lives. They understand the value of establishing a deeper love and commitment to what matters most to them. They take action to develop balance, fulfillment, and their own irresistible magnetism to attract and grow perfect personal and business relationships and opportunities. They do so by partnering with me through my books, seminars, retreats, coaching, and consulting. As they commit to their growth and the transformational processes, they bring forth courage, energy, and focus to their own mission, vision, and desires in life. Thus, they create results for themselves and enthusiastically tell others about my business.

Sandra K. Creech, Ph.D., Teacher, Speaker, Author, Workshop
  Leader
P.O. Box 1447 ✦ Bruceville, Texas 76630
254-718-0655 ✦ skc@templejc.edu

My *mission* is to create an environment where ideas can be brought without judgment and shared without cost, an environment of acceptance.

My *perfect customer* is an organization, individual, or company wanting to achieve more, be more creative, and encourage new ideas for greater profit by creating an accepting environment and using strategic attraction planning as a key to greater success.

Merlyn E. Fance-Douglas
Transformative Technologies
2711 Main Street, Suite 220, Houston, Texas 77002
merlynfance@aol.com

My *mission* is helping organizations, teams, and individuals find and use their buried treasures as a catalyst to help them increase their effectiveness.

My *perfect customers* are organizations, teams, or individuals that want to take their performance to the next level. They are committed to personal growth and development for themselves, their employees, peers, family, and community. They understand how important self-awareness and implementation are to their performance and their contribution to the success of their company, community, and the world. They are dedicated to improving their productivity and responding to change in a positive, powerful, and impactful manner. They view everyone as their customer and are models for how to live and work successfully in today's environment. They expect me to provide them with quality service and sustainable and extraordinary results. They are willing to look for their buried treasures and present them as gifts to others through their performance, achievement, and compassion. We work well together to create a relationship sustained by integrity, commitment, and mutual respect for what each of us brings to the table.

Bob Fenn, Regional Program Manager
Northeast Ohio Procurement Technical Assistance Center —
    Helping Businesses Sell To The Government
Painesville, Ohio ✦ 440-357-2294
bobfenn@lcedc.org ✦ www.lcedc.org/ptac

A Procurement Technical Assistance Center (PTAC) is part of a nation-wide organization funded by the Department of Defense and state and local agencies to help businesses sell their products and services to all levels of government—Federal, state, and local. Everyone knows how maddening it can be to communicate with the government. So why would any business want to bother entering this minefield? Because the Federal government, by itself, is the world's largest customer, spending over $275 billion on goods and services annually. With a PTAC on your side you have enormous expertise to help you in this marketplace.

Our *perfect client* is an established successful business with the talent and product quality to compete in the government sales arena. They have already done some business with the government or a major corporation, and are willing to dedicate the necessary resources and commitment to government sales. They have a people-oriented culture, and will see PTAC as part of their business team. They buy into the fact that government purchases over $800 billion of stuff annually, and don't see why they shouldn't be a part of it. They appreciate the value of our service, and will tell their perfect clients and suppliers about us.

Mary Lynn Fernau, President
The Fernau Group
2705 Maple Lane, Pearland, Texas 77584
281-412-0808 • Ml@thefernaugroup.com

I am a producer. I produce joy, prosperity, and success.

My *perfect customers* are committed to their businesses but value balance in their lives. They are looking for innovative ways to market their business, and they understand the integral part marketing/ PR (public relations) plays in the success of that business. They work with me as a partner—sharing information and triumphs freely. We treat each other with dignity and respect and appreciate each other's expertise. They expect excellence and also provide it. They trust me and pay me well for my expertise. Their appreciation of my work leads them to refer their colleagues and others to me. My perfect customers are top level management who are able to make decisions quickly. They find joy in their work and seeing it succeed.

John Halstead, CEO
Quantum Leap Systems, Inc
Annapolis, Maryland ✦ 410-268-1291
jhalstead@mindspring.com ✦ www.johnhalstead.com

Our *mission* is to provide consultative services, implementation tools, and training to individuals and organizations seeking to create workplaces that thrive and prosper because individuals love their work, value each other, and are committed to shared goals.

Our *perfect customer* is a company or individual seeking to achieve prosperity by making a positive difference in the world and by serving their employees, customers, and vendors equally with truth and love. Our perfect customer is ready to make the shift from things to people, from fear to love, and from breakthrough to continuous improvement. Our perfect customer understands that our relationship is a two-way street consisting of honest communication and feedback, active listening and understanding, and mutual gain. Our perfect customer supports our growth by enthusiastically referring us to others as we do the same for them.

William Alan Hickman, Financial Wellness Consultant, Coach, and
  Mentor
Integrated Wealth Systems, Inc.
P.O. Box 2394, Fairfield, Iowa 52556 ✦ 641-472-1656
ahickman@attracteverything.com ✦ www.attracteverything.com

My *mission* is to help generate peace in the world, by assisting hundreds of millions of people become financially fit and have a more abundant life for themselves, their families, and their communities. Second only to spiritual wellness, financial wellness is the most critical need in our world today. Far more people suffer from poor financial health than any other disease. Helping eliminate the tension created by poor financial health will assist in creating peace and ending terrorism. Using the universal law of attraction, and fundamental financial fitness tools, I help people get out of debt, find their right work, and become financially self-sufficient.

My *perfect customer* is everyone who wants something, and is willing to take action to achieve it.

Charles Howard, Management Consultant, Motivational Speaker
ESP Consulting Services. . . Enhancing Synergistic Performance
Specializing in the development of high performance work environments and cultures
choward@esp-consultants.com • www.esp-consultants.com

Our *mission* is to assist our clients in achieving unparalleled business success by developing the skills needed to create and maintain a cohesive, synergistic, high performance work culture/environment.

Our *perfect clients* are innovative organizations who truly recognize that people are their most valuable resources. They are corporate groups, executives, or teams interested in empowering their human assets and fully leveraging the power inherent in their organization's diversity. They are committed to creating a uniquely positive environment that is cooperative, encouraging, nurturing, and based on service and accountability, and understand that this is the foundation for short and long term business success. Because of that understanding, they are willing to invest in the High Performance Skill (HPS) development of their leaders, knowing that such an investment will give rise to unparalleled creativity, loyalty, and effort on the part of their employees, while at the same time enabling them to most effectively deal with growth and change. Finally, our perfect clients are so pleased and energized by the immediate positive impact of our work that they willingly refer our services to others who can benefit from them.

Kathleen Mierswa, Managing Director
Nine Dots, Inc.   ✦   818-353-7609
ninedotsinc@aol.com   ✦   www.ninedotsinc.com

Our win-win *mission* is to serve as your financial change agent to achieve results out of the box such that you create your dreams of abundance, prosperity, and financial freedom.

Our *perfect clients* are individuals, families, schools, and businesses that desire a reality of success with increased wealth and cash flow. Through our collaboration, you are willing to compensate our Financial Cash Flow trainers, coaches, and consultants to serve as change agents towards achieving your financial freedom. You are responsibly committed to results such that you become more financially literate by taking action after attending our Wealth Thinking and Building sessions and capitalizing on our Financial Literacy seminars. You develop a legacy by giving children a financial head start in the world through our fun-filled Money for Kids workshops. As our perfect client, you are a financial winner living your dreams.

Ellen A. Miller, Business and Life Architect
TEAM Performance   ✦   512-836-2525
12212 Brigadoon Lane, Suite 110, Austin, TX 78727
team@austin.rr.com   ✦   www.makeitabigday.com

Our *mission* is "transforming the workplace by developing trusting and productive teams."

Our *perfect customers* are committed to creating positive business cultures that work, and lives that work powerfully inside those cultures. These organizations see the value of creating results through fun, teamwork, trust, and life-long learning. Together, we design a customized process to meet the specific concerns of your organization. We bring forth honesty, positive spirit, and straightforward communication strategies. Through this empowering partnership, we produce employee fulfillment, extraordinary performance, and bottom-line results.

Joan Portman, Interior Designer, Feng Shui Consultant,
    Inspirational Speaker
Portman Design Associates/Portman Creative Feng Shui
5116 Bissonnet, #306, Bellaire, Texas 77401
713-838-1195 • 713-838-1196 (fax) • joanmport@aol.com

My *mission* is to be a bringer of peace by being an abundant source of balance and harmony through my knowledge and application of the principles of interior design and feng shui.

My *perfect customers* are individuals, entrepreneurs, and corporations committed to personal growth and positive action. Together, we transform their homes and work environments into personal paradises and power centers that attract extraordinary energy. These enhanced environments thus support my perfect clients in achieving their highest goals. In order for us to work effectively, my perfect clients are well paid for the work they do so that they, in turn, pay me at a level that honors the work I do with them. My perfect customers and I respect, honor, and admire one another and naturally refer new and wonderful perfect customers to each other at every opportunity.

C. Olivia Parr Rud
Olivia Group
428 Barker Drive • West Chester, Pennsylvania 19380
610-918-3801 • oliviarud@aol.com

Our *mission* is to assist individuals, groups and corporations in reaching their full potential through self-discovery and personal empowerment.

Our *perfect customer* has the desire to reach their full potential on a personal, financial, and spiritual level. Through coaching, mentoring, and training, our perfect customer learns to enthusiastically take risks, move forward through uncertainty, and savor success. By accessing their inner strength, using their creativity, enhancing their ability to communicate, leveraging the power of cooperation, and learning to embrace change, we facilitate our perfect customer to create their authentic path while embracing their soul purpose. Our services include life and business coaching, training, motivational speaking, and consulting. In select areas, the team at Olivia Group joyously works in cooperation with perfect partners to create an optimal synergy of knowledge and experience.

Robert Sgovio, Integrated Life Systems
Transformational Seminars, Coaching, and
   Healing for Conscious Living
Round Top, Texas • 979-249-5419 • somaflow@cvtv.net

My *mission* is to facilitate individual wholeness and growth by integrating ancient wisdom with the modern world.

My *perfect customers* seek a comprehensive and synergistic approach to personal, professional, and spiritual development. They desire to be fully embodied, connected to themselves emotionally, and are interested in living in a more sacred way. They value and aspire to develop their full potential by honoring and engaging the body, heart, mind, soul, and spirit. They enjoying connecting with people and are in awe of what it means to be a human being. They desire a day-to-day deep and meaningful connection to themselves, their work, and their journey. They value living, learning, and loving.

Monk Simons
M2 Associates
Dallas, Texas • 214-353-2721 • monk_simons@swbell.net

Our *mission* is to have families reinvented, communities revitalized, and youth touched like never before!

Our *perfect customers* are companies in which we increase their revenue model and allow them to expand community relations programs that make a positive impact on the community in which the company is located.

Peggy Swords, CEO

Excalibur Exhibits—Creating unique exhibits and corporate events
with outstanding customer service

Houston, Texas   ◆   713-856-8853

pswords@excaliburexhibits.com   ◆   www.excaliburexhibits.com

Our *mission* is to create unique domestic and international trade show exhibits, corporate events, retail kiosks, and corporate briefing centers that increase the effectiveness of our clients marketing programs through award-winning designs and outstanding customer service.

Our *perfect customer* is a company that believes in the power of three-dimensional marketing and values the return that our innovative designs, teamwork, and pride deliver. Excalibur Exhibits is dedicated to bringing integrity, service, and personalized attention to all our interactions with our customers, vendors, and employees.

Doug Upchurch, CEO

Insights Learning & Development—Austin

Austin, Texas   ◆   512-825-3404

doug@insightsaustin.com   ◆   www.insightsaustin.com

Our *mission* is to work in partnership, supporting you in achieving your goals through self-understanding, individual growth, and a common language for interaction and organizational development.

Our *perfect customer* is a company that believes in finding innovative ways to approach and solve the team and leadership effectiveness problems within their organization. They are looking for a fresh way to help their employees, leaders, and teams communicate and work together more cohesively. They understand that by helping their employees become aware of their own individual styles, they will increase the effectiveness and performance of the organization overall. Our perfect customer works with us to develop a win-win partnership that includes honest feedback, clear vision, and shared values. In working with us, our perfect customers are so pleased with the immediate and positive impact of our work that they willingly tell their colleagues and others about the work we've accomplished together.

Nila Velchoff
Magnetic Radiance
Houston, Texas • 713-501-8974 • velchoff@infohwy.com

My *mission* is to exemplify radiant wellbeing and to train, coach, and inspire others to their fullest potential in the areas of vitality, love, integrity, joy, and consciousness.

My *perfect customers* are individuals committed to aligning their lives with their highest purpose and achieving greater levels of mastery in the areas of wellbeing, love, spirituality, and sacred sexuality. They understand that as they achieve higher levels of love, peace, and wellbeing within themselves, they positively affect the lives of everyone around them and contribute to the greater good of the world. They are coachable, responsible, and enjoy transformational workshops and powerful one-on-one coaching.

Patty Walters, Change Management Consultant
Shell Information Technology International
Houston, Texas • 713-245-3858 • patty.walters@shell.com

My *mission* is to create well-being for teams and leaders while achieving positive quantum-leap results through the establishment of collaborative environments and revolutionary measurements for accountability and effectiveness.

My *perfect customers* are primarily women leaders (Presidents, VPs, Directors, Managers) who desire to be the leaders in creating a new reality in business. They desire to learn a process which will generate immediate, and sustainable, results while impacting the lives of their team members. They desire to motivate and inspire these team mates to reach for goals they never dreamed possible. They are coachable and love to explore different ways of doing business. They create opportunities for a shift in project and leadership models.

Resources

We are pleased to "legacy build" the following list of resourceful organizations and distinguished individuals who have generously contributed their time and energy to ensuring the success of our mission to be the catalysts for a new sales and marketing reality.

If you received a "spark of synchronicity" while reading their philosophies and insights, which are shared throughout this book, please feel free to contact them directly. They look forward to hearing from you.

Additional contact information for these resources will be maintained and updated regularly on PerfectCustomers Unlimited's Web site (www.perfectcustomer.com). Page numbers in parentheses, where provided, indicate where the person or organization is mentioned in this book.

A

Adler, Judy (p. 136)
International Consultant and
 Teacher
Time-Space Feng Shui
Creating A World of Quality
 Living by 2040
www.adlerfengshui.com

Anders, Ann (p. 97)
Vice President Sales and
 Marketing
Yoonite.net
ann@yoonite.net

Antley, Shelly (p. 140)
Vice President—Business
 Development

*Tydeman Dolen . . . Staffing with
 Integrity*
antley@tydemandolen.com

B

Barrett, Richard (p. 18)
Business Consultant, Author
*Richard Barrett and Associates,
 and Corporate Transformation
 Tools*
www.corptools.com

Beckman, Jim (p. 121)
Industrial Ecology, Inc.
info@industrialecology.com

Blakeman, Karen (p. 126)
Interior Architect
kablakeman@lan-inc.com

Notes

1. Geoffrey Brewer, "The Customer Stops Here," *Sales and Marketing Management* (March 1998): 31–34.
2. Rahul Jacob, "Why Some Customers Are More Equal Than Others," *Fortune* (19 September 1994): 215–224.
3. Margaret J. Wheatley and Myron Kellner-Rogers, *A Simpler Way* (San Francisco: Berrett-Koehler Publishers, 1999).
4. Robert Fenn, Ph.D., e-mail message to authors, 12 January 2001.
5. Robert Spector and Patrick D. McCarthy, *The Nordstrom Way* (New York: John Wiley & Sons, 1995).
6. Rick Sidorowicz, "Back to the Beginning—Core Values," *The CEO Refresher*, www.refresher.com/ceo, (18 November 1999).
7. Wayne W. Dyer, *Manifest Your Destiny* (New York: HarperCollins Publishers, 1997).
8. Sarah Ban Breathnach, *Simple Abundance: A Daybook of Comfort and Joy* (New York: Warner Books, 1995).
9. Tom Heuerman, Ph.D., e-mail message to authors, 16 October 2000.
10. Gary Young, e-mail message to authors, 28 June 1999.
11. Kit Lutz, e-mail message to authors, 31 March 2000.
12. J. Richard Stanley, e-mail message to authors, 10 January 2001.
13. George F. Phares, e-mail message to authors, 26 August 1999.
14. Brewer, "The Customer Stops Here," 31–34.
15. Jacob, "Why Some Customers Are More Equal Than Others."
16. Angela Caughlin, e-mail message to authors, 2 September 2000.
17. Jack Canfield, "Self-Esteem and Peak Performance," presentation at Conference on Business and Consciousness, November 1999.
18. Breathnach, *Simple Abundance*.
19. Dyer, *Manifest Your Destiny*, 148.
20. Terri Lewis, e-mail message to authors, 5 September 2000.
21. Merry Mount, e-mail message to authors, 5 September 2000.
22. Michael O'Neal, e-mail message to authors, 22 August 2000.
23. Edwin Young, e-mail message to authors, 9 October 1999.

24. Cynthia Cannizzaro, e-mail message to authors, 8 September 2000.

25. Gary Young, e-mail message to authors, 2 September 2000.

26. Linda Starr, e-mail message to authors, 7 October 1999.

27. Monk Simons, e-mail message to authors, 2 April 2001.

28. Dan Krohn, e-mail message to authors, 5 September 2000.

29. Robert Sgovio, e-mail message to authors, 24 January 2001.

30. Doug Upchurch, e-mail message to authors, 8 April 2001.

31. Ann Anders, e-mail message to authors, 10 January 2001.

32. Evalyn Shea, e-mail message to authors, 12 January 2001.

33. Joan Bolmer, e-mail message to authors, 1 September 2000.

34. Patty Walters, e-mail message to authors, 11 January 2001.

35. Carol Cooper, e-mail message to authors, 4 September 2000.

36. Brewer, "The Customer Stops Here," 31.

37. Ibid.

38. Gem Smith, e-mail message to authors, 7 September 2000.

39. Suzanne Ellis, e-mail message to authors, 3 September 2000.

40. John Clark, e-mail message to authors, 28 July 1999.

41. Rick Crandall, e-mail message to authors, 8 April 2001.

42. Nicole Smart-Wycislo, e-mail message to authors, 1 September 2000.

43. Patricia Rumble, e-mail message to authors, 3 September 2000.

44. Cathy Crawford, e-mail message to authors, 5 April 2001.

45. Jim Beckman, e-mail message to authors, 5 September 2000.

46. Ibid.

47. Zoe Jarboe, e-mail message to authors, 31 August 1999.

48. Robert Stecker, Ph.D., e-mail message to authors, 13 July 2000.

49. Karen Blakeman, e-mail message to authors, 5 September 2000.

50. Jane Boyd, e-mail message to authors, 3 January 2001.

51. Barbara Progar, e-mail message to authors, 12 January 2001.

52. Robert Sgovio, e-mail message to authors, 11 January 2001.

53. Michael Gerber, The E-Myth Revisited (New York: HarperCollins, 1995).

54. Judy Adler, e-mail message to authors, 14 August 2000.

55. Sam Horn, e-mail message to authors, 31 December 1999.

56. Angela Caughlin, e-mail message to authors, 12 January 2001.

57. Shelly Antley, e-mail message to authors, 5 January 2001.

58. Catherine Ponder, *The Dynamic Laws of Prosperity* (Marina del Rey, Calif.: DeVorss & Co., 1985).

59. Heather Leah Smith, e-mail message to authors, 1 September 2000.

60. Lynn W. Ellis, e-mail message to authors, 18 May 2000.

61. Edwin Young, e-mail message to authors, 17 May 2000.

62. Wayne Springer, e-mail message to authors, 17 May 2000.

63. Pamela Grant, e-mail message to authors, 29 June 2000.

64. Toastmasters International Web site home page, www.toastmasters.org.

65. National Speakers Association Web site home page, www.nsaspeaker.org.

66. Suze Orman, *The Courage To Be Rich* (New York: Riverhead Books, 1999.)

67. George Phares, e-mail message to authors, 22 December 1999.

68. Evalyn M. Shea, e-mail message to authors, 16 December 1999.

69. Pamela Terry, e-mail message to authors, 1 September 2000.

70. Florence Scovel Shinn, *The Game of Life and How to Play It* (1925; Reprint, Marina del Rey, Calif.: DeVorss & Co., 1972).

71. Shinn, *The Game of Life and How to Play It*.

Bibliography

Bell, Chip R., and Heather Shea. *Dance Lessons*. San Francisco: Berrett-Koehler Publishers, 1998.

Breathnach, Sarah Ban. *Simple Abundance: A Daybook of Comfort and Joy*. New York: Warner Books, 1995.

Brewer, Geoffrey. "The Customer Stops Here." *Sales and Marketing Management* (March 1998): 31–34.

Day, Laura. *Practical Intuition for Success*. New York: HarperPerennial, 1997.

Dyer, Wayne. *Manifest Your Destiny*. New York: HarperCollins, 1997.

Fike, Linda Kanelakos, and Robert Stecker. *It's U-Mail*. Houston, Tex.: Fike and Stecker, 1996.

Fisher, Donna, and Sandy Vilas. *Power Networking*. Austin, Tex.: Bard Press, 1991.

Gerber, Michael E. *The E-Myth Revisited*. New York: HarperCollins, 1995.

Greenleaf, Robert K. *Servant Leadership: A Journey into the Nature of Legitimate Power and Greatness*. Mahwah, N.J.: Paulist Press, 1977.

Hay, Louise. *You Can Heal Your Life*. Carlsbad, Calif.: Hay House, 1984.

Hendricks, Gay, Ph.D., and Kate Ludeman, Ph.D. *The Corporate Mystic*. New York: Bantam Books, 1996.

Hurley, Kathleen V., and Theodore E. Dobson. *What's My Type? Use of the Enneagram*. San Francisco: HarperSanFrancisco, 1991.

Jacob, Rahul. "Why Some Customers Are More Equal Than Others," *Fortune* (19 September 1994).

Morgen, Sharon Drew. *Selling with Integrity*. San Francisco: Berrett-Koehler Publishers, 1997.

Orman, Suze. *The Courage to Be Rich*. New York: Riverhead Books, 1999.

Ponder, Catherine. *The Dynamic Laws of Prosperity*. Marina del Rey, Calif.: DeVorss & Co., 1985.

Rasmusson, Erika. "The Channels to Watch." *Sales and Marketing Management* (March 1998).

———. "No Advertising? No Kidding!" *Sales and Marketing Management* (September 1998).

Ribadenneira, Diego. "Bringing Your Faith to Work." *Boston Sunday Globe*, 28 March 1999.

Ross, Alan. *The Lure of Lighthouses*. Nashville, Tenn.: Walnut Grove Press, 1999.

Rutte, Martin. "Livelihood: The New Context of Work." Self-published article.

Shinn, Florence Scovel. *The Game of Life*. Marina del Rey, Calif.: Devorss & Co., 1925.

Sidorowicz, Rick. "Back to the Beginning: Core Values." *The CEO Refresher*, www.refresher.com/ceo.html.

Spector, Robert, and Patrick D McCarthy. *The Nordstrom Way: The Inside Story of America's #1 Customer Service Company*. New York: John Wiley & Sons, 1995.

Wheatley, Margaret J., and Myron Kellner-Rogers. *A Simpler Way*. San Francisco: Berrett-Koehler Publishers, 1998.

Index

About the Authors

JAN BROGNIEZ's background includes more than twenty years producing millions of dollars of sales revenue in corporate America. Jan's mastery of strategic planning and her keen business acumen led to the development of Perfect-Customers, Inc.'s proprietary Strategic Design Session process. This

Stacey Hall (left) and Jan Brogniez

process has successfully and effectively empowered a wide variety of corporate executives, entrepreneurs, and sales and operations teams to invent and achieve audacious goals and create organizational legacies in less time than previously has been possible. Called a "pioneer in experiential workshop facilitation," Jan designs and delivers custom-designed workshops, corporate retreats, and executive planning sessions.

As PerfectCustomers, Inc.'s CEO, Jan provides the organizational structure, building the foundation that will sustain the company's unprecedented growth and global presence.

STACEY HALL is credited by industry experts as the inventor and the catalyst for the new Strategic Synchronicity marketing reality. Through this paradigm-shifting methodology, hundreds of corporate executives, entrepreneurs, and sales and training teams have been transformed into powerful magnets that quickly and easily attract the most perfect and profitable customers to their doors and Web sites. Stacey's background includes more than twenty years of designing and implementing global marketing plans for organizations such as FedEx, Budget Rent a Car Corporation, and the University of Houston.

209

As PerfectCustomers, Inc.'s vice president for sales and marketing, Stacey keeps the organization attracting perfect customers and opportunities that are steering the company to success and greater levels of profitability.

PerfectCustomers, Inc., is an experiential consulting and training company whose mission is to be the catalyst for a new reality in the sales and marketing of businesses.

The company was formed when the two cofounders responded to numerous requests to make Strategic Synchronicity available on a global basis.

They share the benefits of Strategic Synchronicity through

- ◆ Synchronicity Leadership Development Program
- ◆ Keynote speeches
- ◆ Experiential presentations
- ◆ Workshops and seminars
- ◆ Corporate retreats
- ◆ "The Daily Strategic Attraction Tip E-zine" (www.perfectcustomer.com)
- ◆ Books published and distributed by Berrett-Koehler Publishers

For more information, contact Jan and Stacey at
info@perfectcustomer.com.

We invite you to participate in our Synchronicity Leadership Program. For more information, please visit our Web site at www. perfectcustomer.com or send an e-mail to info@perfectcustomer.com.

Berrett-Koehler Publishers

Berrett-Koehler is an independent publisher of books, periodicals, and other publications at the leading edge of new thinking and innovative practice on work, business, management, leadership, stewardship, career development, human resources, entrepreneurship, and global sustainability.

Since the company's founding in 1992, we have been committed to supporting the movement toward a more enlightened world of work by publishing books, periodicals, and other publications that help us to integrate our values with our work and work lives, and to create more humane and effective organizations.

We have chosen to focus on the areas of work, business, and organizations, because these are central elements in many people's lives today. Furthermore, the work world is going through tumultuous changes, from the decline of job security to the rise of new structures for organizing people and work. We believe that change is needed at all levels—individual, organizational, community, and global—and our publications address each of these levels.

We seek to create new lenses for understanding organizations, to legitimize topics that people care deeply about but that current business orthodoxy censors or considers secondary to bottom-line concerns, and to uncover new meaning, means, and ends for our work and work lives.

See next pages for other publications from Berrett-Koehler Publishers

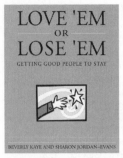

Love 'Em or Lose 'Em
Getting Good People to Stay

Beverly Kaye and Sharon Jordan-Evans

It happens time and time again: the brightest and most talented people leave the company for "better opportunities." Their peers wonder how management could let them go. Their managers feel helpless to make them stay. Beverly Kaye and Sharon Jordan-Evans explore the truth behind the dissatisfactions of many of today's workers and offer 26 strategies—from A to Z—that managers can use to address their concerns and keep them on the team.

Paperback original, 244 pages • ISBN 1-57675-073-6
Item #50736-384 $17.95

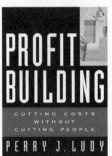

Profit Building
Cutting Costs Without Cutting People

Perry Ludy

Cultivating a loyal, productive workforce is crucial to business success. In *Profit Building,* Perry Ludy—who has worked for top companies in every major field from manufacturing to retail—introduces a five-step process called the PBP (Profit Building Process), which offers specific techniques for improving profitability by stimulating creative thinking and motivating teams to work together more effectively.

Hardcover, 200 pages • ISBN 1-57675-108-2
Item #51082-384 $27.95

Whistle While You Work
Heeding Your Life's Calling

Richard J. Leider and David A. Shapiro

We all have have a calling in life. It needs only to uncovered, not discovered. *Whistle While You Work* makes the uncovering process inspiring and fun. Featuring a unique "Calling Card" exercise—a powerful way to put the whistle in your work—it is a liberating and practical guide that will help you find work that is truly satisfying, deeply fulfilling, and consistent with your deepest values.

Paperback original, 200 pages • ISBN 1-57675-103-1
Item #51031-384 $15.95

Berrett-Koehler Publishers
PO Box 565, Williston, VT 05495-9900
Call toll-free! **800-929-2929** 7 am-12 midnight
Or fax your order to 802-864-7627
For fastest service order online: **www.bkconnection.com**

Fun Works
Creating Places Where People Love to Work

Leslie Yerkes

Leslie Yerkes provides proven tools to unleash the power of fun and make the workplace a winning experience for workers, clients, customers, vendors, and stakeholders alike. It provides a comprehensive set of guiding principles any organization can apply to increase satisfaction and meaning at work by accessing the life-giving force of fun.

Paperback, 200 pages • ISBN 1-57675-154-6 • Item #51546-384 $17.95

301 Ways to Have Fun at Work

Dave Hemsath and Leslie Yerkes
Illustrated by Dan McQuillen

In this entertaining and comprehensive guide, Hemsath and Yerkes show readers how to have fun at work-everyday. Written for anyone who works in any type of organization, 301 Ways to Have Fun at Work provides more than 300 ideas for creating a dynamic, fun-filled work environment.

Paperback, 300 pages • ISBN 1-57675-019-1
Item #50191-384 $14.95

301 More Ways to Have Fun at Work

Dave Hemsath

In this follow-up to the successful *301 Ways to Have Fun at Work*, Dave Hemsath applies the concept to new areas of business life to bring even more fun to the workplace. Like it's predecessor, it combines thorough research with practical hands-on tools for using fun in the workplace to create a more productive and satisfying work environment. Over 300 real-life examples of how individuals and organizations have successfully instilled fun into the workplace make this book immensely practical and fun to read.

Paperback, 255 pages • ISBN 1-57675-118-X
Item #5118X-384 $15.95

Berrett-Koehler Publishers
PO Box 565, Williston, VT 05495-9900
Call toll-free! **800-929-2929** 7 am-12 midnight
Or fax your order to 802-864-7627
For fastest service order online: **www.bkconnection.com**